IMAGES
of America

EARLY
UNIVERSAL CITY

A poster promotes the Victor-Universal release of *Universal City, California*, a four-reel special production that offered newsreel views of the grand opening of "The Strangest Place on Earth." Ten thousand visitors swarmed the Universal lot on this particular opening day—March 15, 1915, and the company has commemorated the date ever since—but Universal City had already been operating for three years, and this was actually the fourth "official" opening ceremony.

ON THE COVER: The camera staff poses in front of the studio film laboratory at Universal City on March 15, 1915.

IMAGES
of America

EARLY
UNIVERSAL CITY

Robert S. Birchard

ARCADIA
PUBLISHING

Published by Arcadia Publishing
Charleston, South Carolina

Printed in the United States of America

Library of Congress Control Number: 2009922893

For all general information contact Arcadia Publishing at:
Telephone 843-853-2070
Fax 843-853-0044
E-mail sales@arcadiapublishing.com
For customer service and orders:
Toll-Free 1-888-313-2665

Visit us on the Internet at www.arcadiapublishing.com

Hopefuls gather at the front gate of Universal City along Lankershim Boulevard in 1916. The Universal Film Manufacturing Company first leased the Oak Crest Ranch from the Hollingsworth family in August 1912. The land was part of the former Providencia Rancho. Universal City moved to its Lankershim Boulevard site in 1914.

CONTENTS

ACKNOWLEDGMENTS

Most of the photographs in this book are from the author's collection. Several additional images were supplied by Marc Wannamaker/Bison Archives, Mark Garrett Cooper, and Mark Vieira/ The Starlight Studio. Special thanks for their help along the way go to Jennifer Dowling, Bob O'Neil, Mike Feinberg, John Murdy, Paul Ginsburg, Ron Roloff, Carla Laemmle, Tracy Terhune, Allan R. Ellenberger, Dennis Dickens, Jerry Roberts, and to those late Universal pioneers who shared their memories with me, including Allan Dwan, Irvin Willat, Edward Sloman, Gilbert Warrenton, Virgil Miller, Ted French, Patsy Ruth Miller, and Beatrice Van.

INTRODUCTION

Universal City is known the world over—as a working movie and television studio and as a tourist destination. The Universal City Studio Tour has been packing them in since the early 1960s, giving visitors a taste of how movies are made leavened with some rollicking amusement park thrill rides and stunt shows to mitigate the drudgery of long working hours and waits between takes that are so much a part of the real world of filmmaking.

The corporate entity that controls Universal City has morphed continuously through its 100-year history—the Independent Moving Pictures Company, the Universal Film Manufacturing Company, Universal Pictures Company, the New Universal, Universal-International, MCA-Universal, Universal Studios, Inc., Vivendi Universal, NBC/Universal—and it must be said that management has not always shown much regard for the company's rich history.

Studio publicity often cites March 15, 1915, as the date of corporate birth—ignoring that Universal City had been in existence for nearly three years and the predecessor companies that created Universal had been around for six years before that date.

Between 1909 and 1930, Universal produced some 5,000 films. Many of them were nickelodeon-era shorts, and separate production numbers for individual serial chapters fattened the title list a bit, but still it was a substantial body of work. In 1948, an earlier regime ordered the destruction of all the studio's silent films to make more space in the vaults. But even as early 1948, only three pre-1920 films were held by the company—*Universal City, California* (1915), *20,000 Leagues Under the Sea* (1916), and *Blind Husband's* (1919). Through its Show-at-Home Library, Universal sold some of its silent titles to 16-mm rental libraries in the 1930s, and a few odd prints have turned up here and there—including a cache buried in an abandoned swimming pool in Dawson City, Canada—but the cinematic legacy of early Universal City survives largely in the form of still photographs, trade journals, and advertising paper.

For much of its early history, Universal was regarded as the "least among equals" of the powerful Hollywood studios. Unlike M-G-M, Paramount, and Fox, Universal did not own extensive theater circuits, nor did its talent roster include many first-rank stars or directors. And often the great talents that did emerge at the studio—Erich von Stroheim, Irving Thalberg, Lon Chaney, John Ford, Clarence Brown, and William Wyler—found greater opportunities and recognition at other companies.

The studio was also ridiculed as a hotbed of nepotism. Studio head Carl Laemmle was famous for hiring his children, cousins, nephews, and family friends for various jobs around the studio. He even set up an egg ranch on the lot to provide work for some relatives who showed little aptitude for the picture business, prompting poet Ogden Nash to quip, "Uncle Carl Laemmle / Has a very large faemmle."

Although most of its pictures were produced on the cheap to cater to independent and small-town exhibitors, Universal often ground out films with little or no regard to cost accounting or whether there was a market for its product. There were several occasions when the company shut down for several weeks to absorb its over-production backlog.

"They had an odd way of budgeting Westerns at Universal in the silent era," recalled director Al Rogell. "They allowed so many dollars for each page of shooting script instead of estimating the actual costs, and they gave the director a bonus for every dollar saved on the budget. I'd get my script writers to write extra pages that would be marked with an asterisk. Universal budgeted on the total number of pages; and, of course I wouldn't shoot the marked pages, and I'd always end up with a nice bonus. Then I'd throw a big party and make sure to invite all the department heads so that if I needed some extra costumes or specially built props they'd charge my picture eight dollars, and tack the rest of the cost onto one of Erich von Stroheim's budgets—and they never figured out how I could make pictures so cheaply."

The mainstay of Universal's output were Westerns with cowboy stars like Hoot Gibson, Jack Hoxie, Tom Mix, Ken Maynard, and Buck Jones; serials like *The Purple Mask* (1917), *The Indians are Coming!* (1930), and *Flash Gordon* (1936) with their cliff-hanging chapter endings; and light comedies starring the likes of Reginald Denny, Glenn Tryon, and the team of Charlie Murray and George Sidney. When Julius Laemmle, renamed Carl Laemmle Jr., was handed the job of studio production head in 1929, Hollywood scoffed and referred to him with the diminutive "Junior Laemmle."

But for all the ridicule, and for all the mediocre pictures ground out along the way, Universal was also innovative. The company had the largest roster of female directors in Hollywood. Many of the studio's self-proclaimed "Super Jewels"—pictures like *Foolish Wives* (1922), *The Hunchback of Notre Dame* (1923), *Smouldering Fires* (1924), *The Phantom of the Opera* (1925), *The Cat and the Canary* (1927), *Lonesome* (1928), and *The Man Who Laughs* (also 1928)—rank among the greatest films of the silent era. Universal also created and became synonymous with the horror film genre through pictures like *Dracula* (1930), *Frankenstein* (1931), and *The Invisible Man* (1933).

Indeed, the studio had much to be proud of. When Hollywood columnist Jimmy Starr suggested that *Frankenstein* was a "freak success" coming out of a "dull" writing staff, Universal scenario editor Richard Schayer shot back, "*Frankenstein* was by no means a 'freak' success. It was carefully planned and carefully produced, designed primarily for box-office. Though every picture we have made has not topped the industry as has *Frankenstein*, most of them have been among the twenty leaders. I point a prehensile finger at *Dracula, East of Borneo, Waterloo Bridge, The Homicide Squad, The Spirit of Notre Dame*. If a dull scenario staff is requisite to produce money-makers of this caliber, then it is a dull scenario staff that Carl Laemmle, Junior and I want to foster."

Carl Laemmle was forced to sell his interest in Universal in 1936 and died three years later. All that survives of the original Universal City buildings is a stained-glass window bearing the Universal logo, which stood above the main entrance of the old administration building. Nevertheless, the property might still be classed as "the strangest place on earth." It is the oldest continually used studio site in Los Angeles and retains an extensive layout of standing sets. For all its seeming shortcomings through the decades, Universal has survived to be one of the most successful of the major Hollywood studios. Although it is impossible to turn back the errors of the past, today NBC/Universal has one of the strongest film preservation programs in Hollywood, and the studio tour has recently added "The Universal Experience," an interactive museum that celebrates the studio's history. The Paris Opera set built for *The Phantom of the Opera* in 1925 is still in use, and many of Universal's soundstages date back to the dawn of sound. If, by some chance, "Uncle Carl" could return to his former domain, he would almost certainly still feel right at home.

One

SHOOTING STAR

Carl Laemmle, the founder of Universal Pictures, emigrated from Germany in 1884 at age 17 and settled in Chicago. He spent more than 20 years as an employee in retail stores working for his wife Recha's father. At age 38, he quit, or was fired, and had only a modest $2,500 nest egg. Laemmle sought out advertising man Robert Cochrane, who suggested he get into a business of his own before the prime of life passed him by. Cochrane thought his former client would invest in another clothing store, but Carl Laemmle had other ideas.

He believed there was money to be made in the movies, but the cautious Cochrane suggested he study the business before investing. Laemmle took Cochrane's advice, learning where films could be obtained, what equipment to use, and what traffic patterns ensured the best potential patronage. On February 24, 1906, Laemmle opened the White Front nickelodeon in Chicago, and within six months he established the Laemmle Film Service, a film exchange that bought prints from producers and rented them to other exhibitors.

As Laemmle's new business became successful, Thomas A. Edison, Inc., formed the Motion Picture Patents Company, seeking to pool the patent interests of leading movie producers and requiring exhibitors to pay a $2 weekly license fee to operate their projectors.

The Patents Company promised to clean up unscrupulous business practices in the industry, but it also threatened to revoke the license of any exchange dealing in unlicensed film. Laemmle perceived this was only the first move in a scheme to ultimately control the film-rental business as well as production and exhibition. He balked at these restrictive measures and declared his independence.

Aided by Cochrane, Laemmle began a weekly barrage of advertisements in the trade magazines, taking the MPPC to task and urging exhibitors to defy the "Trust." This campaign was highly effective, and Laemmle became the spokesman for unlicensed exchange men. As the demand for independent product grew, Laemmle formed Independent Moving Pictures Company (IMP). Their first picture, *Hiawatha*, was released on October 25, 1909.

Theater and film exchange owner Carl Laemmle, pronounced "Lem-ley" (1867–1939), felt threatened when the newly formed Motion Picture Patents Company demanded a $2 weekly license from exhibitors and required that theaters book only films from licensed producers. Unwilling to knuckle under to what he considered extortion, Laemmle began producing his own pictures under the IMP trademark and encouraged other theater owners to go independent.

IMP raided the Biograph Company to hire popular players Florence Lawrence and Mary Pickford, and the Patents Company responded by sending thugs to attack the IMP studio on Fifty-first Street in New York. IMP cameramen hid their cameras under blankets and carried pistols in self-defense as they went on location. Laemmle even sent part of his troupe to Cuba to avoid harassment.

Florence Lawrence, née Florence Annie Bridgwood (1886–1938), began her film career in 1907 with the Vitagraph Company of America but gained widespread, if anonymous, fame as "The Biograph Girl," working with fledgling director D. W. Griffith at the American Mutoscope and Biograph Company in 1908. Film producers of the day refused to divulge actors' names for fear the publicity would lead to escalating salaries. Carl Laemmle lured Lawrence and her husband, Harry Salter, to IMP in 1909 with the promise that her name would be prominently featured in advertisements for her films; then he drummed up a publicity stunt, first suggesting that Biograph announce Lawrence had been killed in a streetcar accident, and then in an advertisement proclaiming "We Nail A Lie," Laemmle revealed that the actress was alive and well and that the missing Biograph Girl was now at IMP.

"King of the Movies" with "A Face as Well Known as The Man in the Moon," King Baggot (1879–1848) signed with IMP in 1909. Typical of many early film stars, Baggot was a working stage actor in stock and touring companies but never a recognized star before he stepped in front of a movie camera. He briefly came to Los Angeles to make pictures for IMP in 1912, but Baggot preferred to live and work in the East, and although Carl Laemmle hoped to consolidate all production in Los Angeles after the formation of Universal, he bowed to Baggot's wishes and maintained eastern production facilities to accommodate the star. Baggot gave up acting for directing in the 1920s, but a fondness for the bottle pushed him back into performing as a bit player and extra in the 1930s.

The song "Shooting Star" was published by the Music House of Laemmle in 1909. Carl Laemmle was in a position to become a multifaceted media mogul but sold his music publishing company in 1912 in order to pursue his battle against the Patents Company and concentrate his efforts on the development of the Universal Film Manufacturing Company.

The IMP stock company is pictured in 1911, before their journey to Cuba to avoid Patents Company harassment. By number, they are (1) Mary Pickford, (2) Owen Moore, (3) King Baggot, (4) Thomas H. Ince, (5) Jack Pickford, (6) Isabel Rae, (7) Lottie Pickford, (8) Joseph Smiley, (9) William Shay, (10) Mrs. David Miles, (11) Joseph MacDonald, (12) Hayward Mack, (13) Mrs. Joseph MacDonald, (14) John Harvey, (15) George Loane Tucker, (16) David Miles, (17) Charlotte Pickford, (18) Robert Daley, and (19) Tony Gaudio.

The original partners in the formation of the Universal Film Manufacturing Company were Carl Laemmle's Independent Moving Pictures Company (IMP), David Horsley's Nestor Film Company, Powers Picture Plays headed by Pat Powers, the New York Motion Picture Company with its widely popular Bison brand films, the Champion Film Company, the Rex Motion Picture Masterpiece Company established by director Edwin S. Porter, and the American branch of the French firm Films Éclair.

Before the Universal City property was acquired, the company opened a ramshackle studio at the southwest corner of Sunset Boulevard and Gower Street in Hollywood; Universal City later used the Sunset-Gower lot as a satellite facility until the late 1910s, when it was turned over to Laemmle relatives Abe and Julius Stern, who produced their Century Comedies on the lot until it was destroyed by fire in 1926. Above is an early shot of Universal's Sunset-Gower studio with an odd bank of light reflectors visible at right. Below, about 1913, Al Christie (with raised arm) directs a scene for one of his Nestor-Universal comedies. Cinematographer Anton Nagy stands behind the camera with assistant Gilbert Warrenton to his right. The muslin sheet over the set diffused the harsh sunlight on the outdoor stage.

Carl Laemmle (right) is seen with Universal's West Coast studio manager, Isidore Bernstein (1876–1944). Although a practicing Jew who cofounded Temple Israel in Los Angeles, Bernstein was invited to join the Hollywood Presbyterian Men's Club in 1913. He also served as the visual inspiration for author Charles E. Van Loan in creating the character of scenario scribe Marcellus M. Peckinpaw, "A little man with glasses and a cough," in the short story "Author! Author!," a part of the Buck Parvin and the Movies series published in the August 1, 1914, issue of *The Saturday Evening Post*. In the story, Peckinpaw becomes a pest who can't be fired because of his ironclad contract with the Titan Studio. Buck Parvin persuades Harvard-educated Indian Peter Lone Wolf to put on paint and feathers and drive Peckinpaw to quit by threatening to scalp him.

Two

GOLDEN OAK RANCH

In 1910, Laemmle's fears were realized when the Patents Company announced the formation of the General Film Company to handle distribution and shut out independent producers and exchanges. The independent producers formed their own distribution alliance, the Motion Picture Distribution and Sales Company, in 1911, but disputes among the members led to its breakup in early 1912. Several of the independents created the Mutual Film Corporation as a cooperative distribution company. In June 1912, the remaining members of the Sales Company regrouped to form the Universal Film Manufacturing Company.

Universal pooled its various production companies, trading shares of Universal stock to the individual company owners and absorbing their interests.

The former heads of New York Motion Picture Company came to resent Universal's intrusion on their independence. They withdrew from Universal and signed with Mutual, taking their popular 101 Bison brand Westerns with them. Universal filed suit to retain the NYMPC interests. The defectors were ultimately allowed to exit Universal but were forced to give up the Bison trademark and $17,000 for the privilege.

In August 1912, Universal leased the Oak Crest Ranch in the San Fernando Valley. In addition to stages and outdoor sets, the company built housing to accommodate 65 families that were permanent residents. An Indian village was also located on the lot. The first official opening of the Universal Oak Crest Ranch occurred on December 3, 1912. Studio grounds were opened to the public, and invitations were sent to state and local politicians and "photoplayers" at other studios.

The second official opening took place on July 10, 1913, when the Universal Oak Crest Ranch was formally named Universal City.

The Universal City Tour had its first incarnation in September 1913, when bus excursions from downtown Los Angeles were initiated.

Weeks after the formation of the Universal Film Manufacturing Company, Adam Kessel and Charles O. Baumann of the New York Motion Picture Company withdrew their 101 Bison brand films. Universal retaliated by attempting to seize Bison's assets. In the final settlement, outlined in the October 16, 1912, "telegram" to exhibitors circulated through the *Moving Picture World* trade magazine, NYMPC was allowed to quit Universal but surrendered the 101 Bison brand name and $17,000.

Form 2289

NIGHT LETTER
THE WESTERN UNION TELEGRAPH COMPANY
INCORPORATED

25,000 OFFICES IN AMERICA   CABLE SERVICE TO ALL THE WORLD

THEO N VAIL, PRESIDENT   BELVIDERE BROOKS, GENERAL MANAGER

RECEIVER'S No.	TIME FILED	CHECK
V.V. 2162	10:30 A.M.	157 PAID

SEND the following NIGHT LETTER subject to
the terms on back hereof which are hereby agreed to   New York City, Oct. 16th, 1912

UNIVERSAL FILM MANUFACTURING COMPANY

1 Union Square, City

THE UNIVERSAL HAS WON. OFFER OF SETTLEMENT MADE BY BAUMANN AND HIS ASSOCIATES HAS BEEN ACCEPTED. New York Motion Picture Co., realizing the victory won by the Universal in the decision of Justice Delany, recently rendered, has assigned all its rights, title and interest in and to the trade marks, trade names and copyrights ''Bison'' and ''101 Bison'' in which assignment all of the stockholders, officers and directors of the New York Motion Picture Co. joined.

Universal Film Manufacturing Company gets the return of all stocks and bonds amounting to nearly one half million dollars, issued to New York Motion Picture Co., and in addition many thousand dollars as damages.

Universal Exchanges exclusively after October 26th will be able to supply ''Bison'' and ''101 Bison'' releases.

This is an unqualified victory for the Universal, considering the hard fight the New York Motion Picture Co., made to retain ''Bison'' and ''101 Bison'' trademarks. Congratulations.

Waldo G. Morse, Attorney.

HELEN CASE
Universal (Bison) Company

From 1912 until Carl Laemmle left the studio in 1936, Universal published a weekly house organ to keep exhibitors apprised of the company's latest releases. *The Universal Weekly*, which was also known at various times as *The Moving Picture Weekly*, was a successor to Laemmle's earlier publication, *The IMPlet*. Universal leading lady Helen Case is featured on the cover of this November 16, 1912, issue.

One of the earliest photographs of Universal City, this was likely taken in late 1912. First leased in August 1912, the Oak Crest Ranch was located north of Hollywood. The first official opening of the Universal Oak Crest Ranch occurred on December 3, 1912.

An aerial photograph of part of Burbank, California, taken about 1940, shows the original Universal City–Oak Crest Ranch location (circled in white) and the back side of the new Universal City lot (outlined in black), which fronts on Lankershim Boulevard (not visible in this picture). Also seen in this photograph are Warner Bros. studio (between the two Universal sites) and the Lake Hollywood reservoir.

On December 3, 1912, the Universal Film Manufacturing Company invited the public to celebrate the opening of its Oak Crest Ranch studio facility. This is a rare snapshot taken that day by one of the attendees.

One of the landmarks of present-day Universal City is the so-called executive "Black Tower," which was built in the mid-1960s. The imposing building makes it clear that people sitting behind the desks are set apart from the rest of the folks who work in the studio. In 1913, the studio offices were less forbidding, and even though a sign on the door said "PRIVATE," the atmosphere was hardly threatening.

Horsepower was still an important factor in transportation in 1913. Cowboys gather in the studio blacksmith shed to get new shoes for their horses. It wasn't just the movie cowboys who kept the blacksmith busy, however. Lumber and other necessities were often hauled around the lot on horse-drawn wagons, and many of the actors and other personnel "drove" to work on horseback.

Animals were also a factor in picture making, and Universal maintained its own zoo to meet the requirements of movie scenarios. The handful of sheep and one pig in this 1913 photograph of the studio menagerie would not make Noah jealous, but Universal's zoo would eventually be home to a wide assortment of animals, including an elephant.

Two views of the Carriage Painting Department at Universal City in early 1913 are presented here. It was often necessary to modify vehicles to fit the needs of the films in production. The chariot, which has the words "BEN-HUR Ocean Park" painted on the side, was acquired from an attraction in that beachside community and here awaits repainting for use in the movies.

This is the Universal City prop shop in 1913. Here pieces needed for films could be made or modified to suit production needs. Standing to the left of the shop are plaster statues of "Blind Justice" and a Roman centurion—suggesting the range of stories and eras the prop makers might need to address in their work.

Although many of the earliest buildings on the Universal City lot were rather crude in their construction, the studio commissary was as well appointed as any store on Main Street, U.S.A., at the time. On this side of the restaurant are a cigar stand, a soda fountain, and a confection counter.

Although Universal took photographs of studio buildings to show off its new facility to the trade and potential outside renters, few surviving photographs exist of work on the studio's first outdoor stages. These next several pictures are snapshots taken by visitors to Universal City in late 1912. Above is the newly constructed Western street. If the sets look somewhat modest, it must be remembered that one- and two-reel films, which ran from 15 to 30 minutes, were budgeted at between $500 and $1,500. Money wasn't available to lavish on sets. Below is a view of one of Universal City's first two outdoor stages with attached prop room. The long building is a barracks. Over 70 people lived full- or part-time on the lot by 1913.

Above, a unit was working on the second stage shooting interiors for a Western picture when visitors came to the Oak Crest Ranch. Part of the property's appeal for Universal was the scenery, with the Los Angeles River next to the lot and mountains and desert nearby. Ideal for making movies, the property was thought by Carl Laemmle to be too small. He decided to acquire a larger tract along Lankershim Boulevard. The first Universal City site would eventually become the Jesse L. Lasky Feature Film Company Ranch. Below is a closer angle on the stage. A horse wagon delivers needed supplies, and the cameraman is just visible behind the horse, wearing a cap and carrying a box of equipment. The camera stands unmanned at the edge of the stage.

An unidentified cinematographer poses for the visitors between takes. It was common in the nickelodeon era for each scene to play in a single shot. Most American cameramen worked closer to the actors, with the camera view cutting just below the actors' knees. Such framing was known as "American foreground." European filmmakers tended to keep the actor in the frame from head to toe, which was known as "French foreground" staging.

This photograph gives an idea of how deep the stage floor was. The cameraman working on the stage in the background is using a crude reflector made of muslin stretched on a wooden frame to pump sunlight under the actors' hat brims to make their faces more visible. The actor playing an Indian in the foreground is slathered in "Bolemany" (Bole Armenia), a skin-darkening makeup used to suggest instant, if not realistic, ethnicity.

This cavalry fort was built in December 1912. It is a rather odd-looking structure with its low walls and Spanish tile atop the peaked roofs of the front gate guardhouses, but for the unquestioning audiences of the time, it served to evoke the sort of Western outposts they had read about in *Buffalo Bill Weekly*, *Wild West Weekly*, *Diamond Dick Weekly*, and other Western-themed dime novel adventures.

The Range Deadline (Nestor-Universal, released July 2, 1913) told the well-worn story of cattleman versus sheep man, with young lovers Sheriff Dave (center foreground) and Edna Mabrey, the sheep rancher's daughter, caught in the middle. Dave was played by Lawrence Peyton (1895–1918), whose career was cut short when he was killed in action during World War I. Edna was played by Helen Case (1885–1977).

In another scene from *The Range Deadline*, Sheriff Dave (Lawrence Peyton) slaps some handcuffs on one of cattle rancher Jim Hall's henchman. Noble Johnson played the mustachioed villain. Johnson (1881–1978) was a light-skinned black man who had a long and wide-ranging career. As here, he often passed for white on screen, but he also played Indians, Mexicans, and other ethnic types and is perhaps best remembered for his role as a native chief in *King Kong* (Radio Pictures, 1933). Johnson would also go on to establish the Lincoln Motion Picture Company, the first black-owned production company, in 1915 with financial backing from actor Harry Carey. Lincoln's first release was titled *The Realization of a Negro's Ambition*, in which the black hero ended up with a gushing oil well at the climax of his adventures.

Princess Mona Darkfeather (1882–1977) was trumpeted as a full-blooded Seminole Indian when she first appeared in pictures for the Bison Company in 1909. Later, when she sought to diversify her screen portrayals, she merely claimed to be "of Spanish descent." In fact, her real name was Josephine M. Workman, born in the Boyle Heights neighborhood of Los Angeles. Darkfeather and her husband, actor-director Frank Montgomery (1870–1944), signed with Universal in late 1912 and stayed with the company for a year, turning out films like *Darkfeather's Sacrifice* and *Juanita* before setting up their own production company, which released pictures through the Kalem Company. Darkfeather was director Cecil B. DeMille's first choice for the role of Nat-U-Rich in his famed 1914 feature debut *The Squaw Man*, but she was unavailable and the role went to Red Wing (Lillian St. Cyr).

The Violet Bride (Powers-Universal, released May 14, 1913) featured, from left to right, Edith Bostwick, Jeanie Macpherson, and Harry von Meter. Macpherson (1887–1946) began her screen career at the Biograph Company in 1908. Her tenure at Universal City began in 1913 and lasted barely a year. She later became director Cecil B. DeMille's favorite screenwriter, penning films like *Male and Female* (1919), *The Ten Commandments* (1923), and *The King of Kings* (1927).

THE MOTION PICTURE STORY MAGAZINE

15 CENTS

AUGUST

AUGUSTUS CARNEY (ESSANAY)

Augustus Carney, on the August 1913 cover of *Motion Picture Story*, gained screen fame in *Alkali Ike's Auto* (Essanay, 1911) and played Alkali Ike in numerous Snakeville Comedies produced by Essanay in Niles, California. When he was hired by Universal in 1914, the studio hoped to inherit Carney's screen character, but Essanay claimed ownership, and Carney became "Universal Ike" in the 15 pictures he made for Carl Laemmle.

By far, the most popular comedians on the Universal roster were Eddie Lyons (1886–1926) and Lee Moran (1888–1961), who starred together at Universal for nearly 10 years on and off. This is a scene from one of their early efforts, *The Battle of Bull Con* (Nestor-Universal, released September 19, 1913), directed by Al Christie, who first hired the pair for the Nestor Film Company in 1911. Russell Bassett stands in the middle at the top of the steps. In the foreground, from left to right, are Ramona Langley, Moran, Donald MacDonald, and Lyons. Universal's comedy units commonly parodied the studio's popular dramatic films, and this one-reeler poked good-humored fun at *The Battle of Bull Run* (released March 18, 1913), a two-reel Civil War drama directed by Francis Ford and starring Grace Cunard and William Clifford.

Three

THE STRANGEST PLACE ON EARTH

In February 1914, Universal started planning its new studio facility along Lankershim Boulevard, which included the former Taylor, Boag, Davis, and Hershey ranches.

Universal City's third grand opening occurred on October 14, 1914. This event was for employees and was occasioned by a visit from Laemmle, who announced that the official "Official Opening" would occur on February 2, 1915. This date was eventually extended to March 15 when it was determined that the facilities would not be ready by February.

The ultimate celebration of Universal City's "grand opening" began in Chicago, where company executives, exchange men, exhibitors, and trade reporters gathered at the Hotel Sherman on March 7 before boarding a train for Los Angeles. The Universal train pulled into San Bernardino on Saturday, March 13, and the entourage visited Busch Gardens in Pasadena on March 14.

After Laemmle opened the Universal City gate on March 15, an estimated 10,000 visitors were treated to festivities that included numerous staged moviemaking exhibitions. A planned air battle was put off until Tuesday when pilot Frank Stites failed to get his plane off the ground after finding the air "too light to lift its bulk."

Tragedy struck the next day when Stites again attempted his air stunt. A dummy airplane was suspended on a wire between two hills, and Stites made several passes. At the signal of a director on the ground, he was to buzz the mock enemy plane and drop a prop bomb. The replica plane moving along the wire was filled with explosives that were set off as Stites's bomb of cloth and twine fell. In the concussion from the explosion, Stites lost control of his plane, which plunged into freefall. He attempted to jump to safety but did not survive the 60-foot fall.

Stites's death brought an abrupt end to the opening celebrations at Universal City. The guests who had made the cross-country train trip left Los Angeles ahead of schedule and ended their junket with a visit to the Panama-Pacific Exhibition in San Francisco.

In February 1914, William Horsley was put in charge of supervising construction of administration and laboratory buildings at the new Universal City, and ground-breaking for the permanent buildings took place on June 8. By August, foundations for the permanent buildings had been laid and framing was underway. In October, it was reported that 500 people lived at Universal City—425 in cottages, and the other 75, all Indians, in teepees on the back lot.

Universal City's third grand opening occurred on October 14, 1914. This event was for employees and was occasioned by a visit from Carl Laemmle, who announced that the official "Official Opening" would occur on February 2, 1915. This date was eventually extended to March 15 when it was determined that the facilities would not be ready by February. This photograph shows the back lot as it looked in January 1915.

The new administration building is shown in late 1914 before landscaping had been completed, with the film laboratory in the background. The first structures at Oak Crest Ranch had been erected well away from traffic and prying eyes, but these buildings fronted on Lankershim Boulevard, a dirt road that would become a major thoroughfare. The circular stained-glass window above the entrance is all that survives of the original Universal City buildings.

John "Alaska Jack" Giniva appears at the Majestic Theater in an unidentified town in February 1915, showing "moving pictures of the Arctic region with lecture." Also on the bill is *The Country Boy*, a film produced by the Jesse L. Lasky Feature Play Company. In addition, the theater is promoting a contest in which an entrant will win a free trip to Universal City and appear in a movie.

The celebration of Universal City's "grand opening" actually began in Chicago, where company executives, exchange men, exhibitors, and trade reporters gathered at the Hotel Sherman on March 7, 1915, before boarding a special train consisting of four compartment cars, a diner, buffet, and drawing room car for a scenic tour to Los Angeles. Above, Carl Laemmle doffs his hat to well-wishers at the Dearborn Station before boarding the train. Below, P. A. "Pat" Powers (1896–1948), who controlled a 40-percent stake in Universal, was described by historian Terry Ramsaye as being "one of the most belligerently active men in the [motion picture] industry." Outwardly friendly, Powers and Laemmle waged a bitter rivalry for control of Universal, which ended in 1920 when Laemmle bought Powers's shares.

The cross-country trip to Universal City was documented in still photographs and motion pictures by cameraman U. K. Whipple, a cinematographer with the company's newsreel division, the *Universal Animated Weekly*. Above, the crowd bids farewell to the picture people as they begin their seven-day cross-country trip to "the strangest city in the world." Below, on the rear platform of the observation car, the "Universalites," as they were called, anticipate their journey. In the group are P. A. Powers (second from left); distribution manager M. H. Hoffman (holding derby); Carl Laemmle's wife, Recha (fourth from right); their son Julius Laemmle; chief editor Joseph "Jack" Brandt (second from right); and Carl Laemmle.

The first stop on the junket to Universal City was Kansas City. All along the route, the Universal publicity department made sure that crowds greeted the travelers—even when the weather was not conducive to high spirits. Above, the snow on the ground did not dampen the enthusiasm of these Kansas City folks. Below, Jack Brandt left the Universal City–bound train in Kansas City and here offers a farewell handshake to Carl Laemmle. Brandt (1882–1939) would later partner with Harry and Jack Cohn to form C.B.C Film Sales (Cohn, Brandt, and Cohn)—often referred to derisively among industry insiders as "Corned Beef and Cabbage." C.B.C Film Sales became Columbia Pictures in January 1924 and overcame its "poverty row" origins to become a major Hollywood studio.

Above, after stopping in Denver, Colorado, the Universal train laid over in Albuquerque, New Mexico, where Laemmle and his companions called on the Universal Theater, a nickelodeon that booked the Universal program. It was common for theaters in this era to run three short films and change bills daily. Universal ground out pictures at a furious pace to feed this market. While in Albuquerque, the group visited a Pueblo Indian village and had a banquet at the Savoy Hotel. Below, perhaps because they rebelled against the Motion Picture Patents Company, Carl Laemmle (right) and Pat Powers (center) took special pleasure in meeting Confederate rebel icon Henry Saxon Farley. Farley resigned from West Point in November 1860 to join the 1st South Carolina Artillery and ordered the first shots fired against Fort Sumter on April 12, 1861, initiating the Civil War.

Above, another icon of American history who greeted the Universalites in Albuquerque was William F. "Buffalo Bill" Cody (1846–1917), Western scout and buffalo hunter, who gained lasting fame when he established Buffalo Bill's Wild West in 1883. The circus-like show, which featured real cowboys and Indians performing rodeo turns and re-creations of stagecoach holdups and the Indian Wars, toured the United States and Europe for over 40 years. Pat Powers (left) had been involved in *The Life of Buffalo Bill*, a 1912 three-reel special attraction. Below, after another stopover at the Grand Canyon in Arizona, the Universal train pulled into San Bernardino, California, on Saturday, March 13, 1915. The following day, the troupe visited Busch Gardens in Pasadena before arriving at Universal City on March 15.

Above, the Universalites stop to chat as they move up the platform toward the welcoming festivities at the Santa Fe station in Los Angeles. Below, after six days riding on the train and sightseeing along the way, the movie folk broke into a spontaneous dance to the strains of guitar and ukulele music. *The Los Angeles Times* reported, "At the Santa Fe station here, the entire population of Universal City Indians, band, cowboys and actors and actresses were gathered in welcoming enthusiasm and small arm salvos and a ukulele chorus accomplished a tantrum of noise that brought all East First Street to the fore."

Above, Universal City chief of police Laura Oakley (1879–1957) awaits the arrival of the Universalites on Monday morning, March 15, 1915. Oakley was elected police chief in June 1913. There were some 300 permanent residents and more than 1,000 transients on some working days at Universal City, and 700 votes were cast. Studio manager A. M. Kennedy was elected mayor, actress Grace Cunard won the title of city assessor, actor Wallace Reid was street commissioner, and director Allan Dwan became head of the censor board. California granted women the right to vote by referendum in 1911, and suffragettes won 10 of the 28 Universal City offices. Still, the posts were honorary and perhaps even a bit capricious—despite its name, Universal City has never actually been incorporated as a municipality. Below, Carl Laemmle and his companions stroll up Lankershim Boulevard toward the Universal City gate.

Above, Laura Oakley towers over the 5-foot, 3-inch Carl Laemmle as she presents him the key to Universal City, though undoubtedly she's standing on a raised platform. The dark-haired man behind and to the left of Carl Laemmle is his brother-in-law, Maurice Fleckles (1871–1946), who was married to Carl's sister Anna. Although Pat Powers (partially obscured behind Laura Oakley) is smiling in most of the photographs taken of the Universal City cross-country journey, his scowl in this photograph more clearly reflects his behind-the-scenes relationship with Carl Laemmle. Below, as quickly as the official still photographer snapped photographs, it wasn't possible to "point and shoot" with the bulky 5-by-7-inch film camera he used, so Carl Laemmle's wistful reaction to receiving the key to Universal City was re-created after the fact.

At left, Carl Laemmle joins in cheering himself and his fellow Universalites as he prepares to unlock the gate to the "strangest city in the world." Below, the photographer made a point of getting a well-posed shot of Carl Laemmle placing the key in the lock. Of course, from the people visible on the outer side of the gate, it is clear that even on this ceremonial occasion "Uncle Carl" was not actually the first one inside on March 15, 1915. As with every other phase of the grand opening tour, each moment of the opening ceremony was carefully planned to achieve the greatest publicity impact.

Publicity was the goal of the gala Universal City opening, and the ceremony was a wild success. Newspapers and trade magazines gave the event extensive coverage, and newsreel footage was circulated in theaters across the country. "Once inside the gate," wrote *Los Angeles Times* reporter Grace Kingsley, "gaily clad Universal girls pelted the crowd with flowers, and a big cavalcade of mounted cowboys and Indians in their war paint saluted with pistol shots and war dances, bands played, and Pat Powers, treasurer of Universal, hoisted the huge American flag followed by a display of daylight fireworks." From these photographs of Carl Laemmle and Isidore Bernstein entering the studio walking up Laemmle Drive, it seems that plenty of men tossed posies as well.

After the gates of Universal City opened to the public, a reception was held for invited guests. Above, from left to right in the foreground, are Isidore Bernstein, Carl Laemmle, Ola Humphrey, and actress Edna Maison. Universal touted the fact that a Turkish princess attended. Humphrey (1876–1848) was indeed a princess by marriage—the estranged wife of Ibrahim Hassan, cousin of the Khedive of Egypt—but she was born in San Francisco, the daughter of a furniture salesman, and had an extensive career as a stage actress before she married Hassan. She was making an autobiographical film, called *Under the Crescent*, for Universal at the time. Below, from left to right in the foreground, are director Otis Turner, Isidore Bernstein, Carl Laemmle, and actress Ann Little. Pat Powers and Robert Cochrane stand behind Laemmle.

After a toast to the success of Universal City, more speeches were made about the success of Universal City. For the VIPs, Carl Laemmle seemed unwilling to speak off the cuff, and his well-chosen remarks were committed to paper before delivery to the assembly. Below, Pat Powers is relegated to the background as Laemmle is flanked by West Coast manager Isidore Bernstein on the left and Robert H. Cochrane (1879–1973) in the white suit on the right. Cochrane was the Chicago advertising man who handled the account for the clothing store owned by Carl Laemmle's father-in-law. Cochrane had suggested that Laemmle get into a business of his own, and he made Laemmle a well-known figure by ghostwriting the "straight talk to exhibitors" pieces that appeared regularly in Universal trade advertisements.

Charles Rosher (1885–1974) was one of 15 Universal City cinematographers in 1915. Born in London, England, he was an assistant to Richard Speaight, photographer for the British Crown. Rosher came to the States to show his photographs and brought a movie camera with him. In 1910, David Horsley offered Rosher a job with his Nestor Film Company. When Universal absorbed Nestor, Rosher went along. He later became Mary Pickford's favorite cameraman.

After this photograph was snapped, these cameramen fanned out across Universal City to cover the opening day festivities. From left to right are (kneeling) chief cameraman Lee Bartholomew and superintendant of the laboratory William C. Foster; (standing) Al Cawood, Fred LeRoy Granville, Anton Nagy, Steve Rounds, Friend Baker, Eddie Ullman, Al Siegler, Oscar G. Hill, Charles Rosher, R. E. Irish, Ralph Merollo, Steve Norton, and Park Reis.

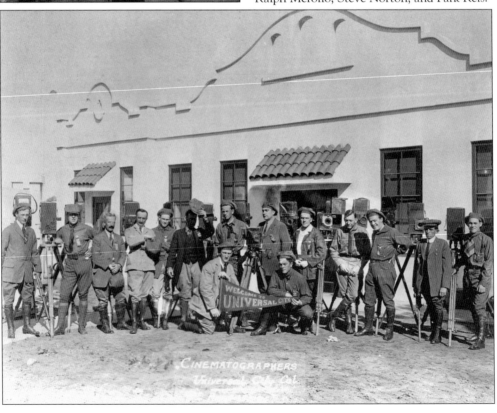

Carl Laemmle pauses for a "Kodak moment" with his son, six-year-old Julius Laemmle, outside the Universal City administration building on March 15, 1915. Julius would later use the name Carl Laemmle Jr. and was put in charge of production at Universal when he reached the age of 21.

The Laemmle family poses for a more formal opening day portrait. From left to right are (seated) Recha (Mrs. Carl) Laemmle, Julius Laemmle, and Carl Laemmle; (standing) Carl Laemmle's brother Louis Laemmle, their sister Anna Laemmle Fleckles, and their brother-in-law Maurice Fleckles.

Above, more than 500 cars are parked at Universal City on opening day, an astounding figure much emphasized in publicity—but, in fact, 1915 was well before Los Angeles was a city on wheels. The estimated opening day crowd was 10,000, and most arrived by bus. This photograph looks northwest into the largely undeveloped San Fernando Valley. This angle also offers a view of the back side of the big outdoor stage, with offices and two rows of dressing rooms behind. The building with the barrier fence around it to the left of the two large trees is the new, yet-to-be-completed, studio commissary. The sign, which reads, "THE GREAT HASH MYSTERY," pokes fun at the July 1914 Universal release *The Great Universal Mystery*. Below, opening day visitors swarm onto the lot.

Above, the big stage at Universal was said to be able to accommodate as many as 16 different production units working side-by-side at one time. Universal began experimenting with using artificial light to shoot movies as early as 1913, when studio electrician, and later cinematographer, Virgil Miller began shooting tests with mercury vapor lamps on a small "dark" stage. However, sunlight still provided the main source of illumination for Universal pictures in 1915. Below, Universal actors, directors, and crew members put on moviemaking expositions all day long on opening day, and the throngs of visitors were able to catch glimpses of their screen favorites in action. Most of the day's "work" was for show, but some of the footage reached the screen in such promotional films as *Universal City, California* (Victor-Universal, 1915) and *Behind the Scenes* (Nestor-Universal, 1915).

Above, visitors watch Al Christie, in the dark suit and hat right of the camera, direct a comedy scene. Anton Nagy is the cameraman, and Eddie Lyons is the pistol-toting young man shooting up the apartment hotel. To save money, filmmakers erected only sets seen on screen. The wall to the left of the stairs and second floor landing were deemed unnecessary for this camera setup. Some of Nagy's footage, as well as footage shot by another cameraman of Christie and Nagy at work, was incorporated in the two-reel film *Behind the Scenes* (Nestor-Universal, 1915). Cinematographer Charles G. Clarke found one reel of this film while on location in Alaska. It is the only known surviving footage of Universal City's opening festivities. Below is another view of the crowd reviewing the filmmaking demonstrations on the big stage.

The studio caption reads, "J. Warren Kerrigan and the man who discovered and made him." In fact, Kerrigan began his movie career at the Essanay Company in Chicago in 1910. He was lured away by the American Film Company later that year and was voted the most popular motion picture star in a 1912 *Photoplay* magazine poll before he signed with Carl Laemmle in 1913.

The team of Francis Ford and Grace Cunard wrote, directed, and starred in Universal's first serial, *Lucille Love, The Girl of Mystery* (1914), and here they are about to start *The Broken Coin* and take a location jaunt to Tijuana. Francis Ford (in white hat) leans against the camera. Harry Schumm stands behind Ford to the right, and E. M. Keller stands third from left. Grace Cunard sits in front of the camera.

Above, the crowd moves toward the Universal City back lot for the rest of the day's entertainment, passing the remnants of past films. Visible on the hill are a small castle and a cabin front. The building to the right is the scene dock where set pieces were stored for reuse, and the frame structure in front of the scene dock was used to hang backing canvases for scenic paintings. Below, this Indian tepee was a movie set piece, but there were a number of Indians who lived at Universal City and worked in the studio's Westerns.

Above, Carl Laemmle pays a call on his Native American employees. A number of Indians lived on the lot in the early days at Universal City. Typically, because they did not care to be away from home for long, the Native Americans stayed at the studio for several months and returned to their reservations when rotating replacements arrived. Below, the Western stunt show begins with Universal's Indian tribe attacking a stagecoach. With the stage driver in white shirt and snap-brim cap, it is clear that this action was intended only for the amusement of the opening day visitors and not for the movie screen.

The most spectacular portion of the opening day entertainment at Universal City revolved around a staged Indian raid on a small Western village (above). Cowboys ride to the rescue with guns blazing (below), but the Indians are intent on dynamiting the earthen dam on the hill and flooding the town. Even though there were a number of motion picture and still cameras trained on the action, the images were never intended to be used in any of the studio's Western movies. The attendees scattered over the surrounding hills to get a good view, making it impossible for the cameramen to get "clean" shots of the action, but the scenes were included in the newsreel release *Universal City, California*.

Above, a dynamite charge exploded and the dam collapsed, sending a cascade of water down the hill toward the town. Below, the heroine races from the torrent as the floodwaters destroy a mining camp's small buildings. One of the studio's still cameramen and his assistant are visible at the left photographing with the sort of bulky view camera common at the time. Stills were shot with large format cameras, using 5-by-7-inch, 6-by-9-inch, or 8-by-10-inch film or glass-plate negatives, making contact prints possible without the trouble or expense of making enlargements.

Above, a snapshot view of the same action as on the previous page was taken at almost the same precise moment as the water floods the bridge and heads for a drainage ditch. Below, in the aftermath of the flood action, director Henry McRae (on horseback) rides away from the scene. Cinematographers Fred LeRoy Granville, Allen Siegler (center), and Friend Baker are in the back of the automobile after shooting the scene. Granville is holding a small still camera and may have shot the image above. In the background, the backs of Tudor-style sets are juxtaposed against the facade of a Russian Orthodox church, justifying Universal City's reputation as "the strangest place on earth." Such odd back lot juxtapositions may well have inspired the eclectic architecture that flourished in Los Angeles in the 1920s and 1930s.

The public portion of the opening day celebration ended and the crowd drifted back toward the front gate. One promised attraction did not take place on March 15. Pilot Frank Stites was to have performed some aerobatic stunts in his biplane. The air battle was delayed until Tuesday, after Stites found the air "too light to lift its bulk," meaning the plane. Stites felt he needed to emulate the aerobatic exploits of Curtiss Exhibition Flying Team member Lincoln Beachey if he was to stay a competitive flyer. Ironically, Beachey was killed on March 14, when the wings of his plane broke away as he dove into San Francisco Bay.

Above, visitors on Tuesday, March 16, 1915, were treated to a rodeo contest. Cowboys were an important part of picture making in the early days. Not only were Western films popular with audiences, but the rough-and-tumble wranglers were also the first movie stuntmen. Day players were hired when needed, but Universal kept about 30 cowboys on the payroll to work in pictures and "stable around" when they weren't in front of the cameras. "It was real glamorous," recalled cowboy Ted French. "We shoveled an awful lot of horse shit." Below, cinematographer Allen G. Siegler (1892–1960) dazzles the crowd with some plain and fancy roping; he began his film career as a cowboy with the Vitagraph Company in 1911.

Henry McRae and Julius Laemmle pose on horseback before the rodeo. McRae (1876–1944) was an ally of Carl Laemmle in his behind-the-scenes battles with Pat Powers and was named director-general at Universal City, which meant, in theory, that he supervised other directors on the lot. A prolific filmmaker, he directed more than 130 films between 1912 and 1932, but he was hardly an inspired one. He became head of Universal's serial unit in the late 1920s and supervised such chapter plays as *The Indians Are Coming!* (1930), *Flash Gordon* (1936), and *The Green Hornet* (1940). Born in Canada, McRae claimed to have been a member of the Royal Mounted Police and was sufficiently comfortable around animals to allow himself to be roped off the back of a donkey during the rodeo.

Ever on the lookout for a way to promote himself, Carl Laemmle had these pictures taken on Tuesday, March 16, as Frank Stites prepared to make good on his failed flight attempt of the day before. The still photographer framed these shots at such an angle, from below looking up, as to suggest that Laemmle was actually in the air with the pilot. Fortunately, Laemmle kept his feet firmly planted on the ground as Stites took to the sky. With Universal executives and a crowd of more than 1,000 waiting for the flight on Tuesday, Stites told his assistant he had no choice but to go up, even as his shock over Lincoln Beachey's death made him reluctant to carry out the acrobatic stunts he had been hired to perform.

A dummy airplane was suspended on a wire above the ground between two hills, and Frank Stites made several passes around it. Then, at the signal of a director on the ground, he was to buzz the mock enemy plane and drop a prop bomb. The replica plane moving along the wire was filled with explosives that were set off as Stites's cloth-and-twine bomb fell. In the concussion from the explosion, Stites lost control of his plane, which plunged into freefall. He attempted to jump to safety but did not survive the 60-foot fall. The pilot's death brought an abrupt end to the opening celebrations at Universal City. The guests who had made the cross-country train trip left Los Angeles ahead of schedule, ending their junket at the Panama-Pacific Exhibition in San Francisco.

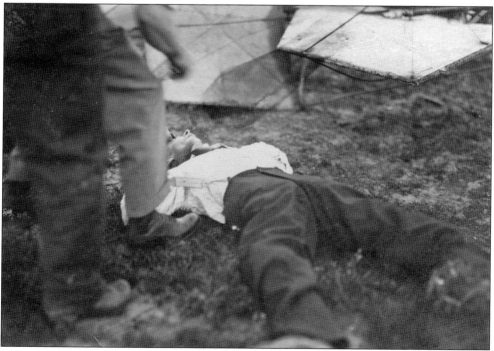

Carl Laemmle speaks to guests at a St. Patrick's Day party hosted by Pat Powers at the Alexandria Hotel in downtown Los Angeles. Although the death of Frank Stites the day before ended celebrations at the studio, Powers went ahead with this March 17, 1915, gathering. Seated on the dais behind Laemmle are Universal star J. Warren Kerrigan (wearing party hat); party host P. A. "Pat" Powers, who was born in Waterford, Ireland; and Isidore Bernstein (wearing glasses). Below, the attention of the banquet crowd is directed away from the dais, which is in the background at left, for some unknown distraction. Visible among the crowd, at the third table back on the right, are Laura Oakley, Francis Ford, and Grace Cunard. Victoria Forde is seated at the next table back, directly behind Cunard.

Four

A GOOD CAST
IS WORTH REPEATING

One phrase that sticks in the mind of anyone who has seen a Universal picture from the 1920s or early 1930s is the declaration on the end credit list that "A Good Cast Is Worth Repeating." There was also a variation used occasionally that insisted "A Universal Cast Is Worth Repeating." Few could argue with the first proposition, but some might dispute the second.

During his tenure as the head of studio, it has to be said that Carl Laemmle never seemed to be able to develop a roster of contract talent that would propel Universal pictures into the "must see" category for starstruck fans.

Not that he didn't try. In Universal's early years, it seemed obsessed with raiding other studios for their already established stars—Florence Lawrence, Mary Pickford, J. Warren Kerrigan, Augustus "Alkali Ike" Carney, Ford Sterling, Hobart Bosworth—all were picked off by Universal after their popularity was established elsewhere. Yet even when Universal acquired established stars, the company didn't seem to know what to do with them. Only Kerrigan, among those listed above, stayed at the studio for more than a year.

Even in developing fresh talent, the studio never seemed to get it right—Lon Chaney, Francis Ford, Grace Cunard, Jack Hoxie, and others all seemed to ignore their better natures and clashed with Universal management.

Universal did have a group of reliable performers, but they were not generally among the top box-office performers. M-G-M, for example, had Greta Garbo, Norma Shearer, John Gilbert, Joan Crawford, William Powell, Jean Harlow, Myrna Loy—"more stars than there are in heaven," as M-G-M flacks were proud to shout. Universal had Reginald Denny, Laura La Plante, Hoot Gibson, Cullen Landis, Mary Philbin, John Boles, Sidney Fox, Norman Kerry, and Lew Ayres. Often, when Universal was casting one of its big pictures, it would go to other studios for a "loan out" of one of their stars or relied on freelance talent that might as easily add to the luster of a Columbia Picture or a United Artists film when not toiling at Universal City. But even with limited star power, Universal managed to turn out a number of screen classics that have remained in the popular imagination much longer than some of the star vehicles produced at other studios.

Universal patted itself on the back with *The Great Universal Mystery* (Nestor-Universal, released July 10, 1914), an all-star extravaganza that showed off most of the actors and directors on its roster. This scene, featuring J. Warren Kerrigan garbed as a Roman centurion, is symbolic of all the time frames and characters the movies can bring to audiences. The "monkey man" with beard and crown to the left of Kerrigan is said to be Lon Chaney. When director Allan Dwan started a second production unit, featuring Wallace Reid, at the Flying A studio in Santa Barbara in 1913, Kerrigan threatened to quit, so Dwan was fired. After Dwan was hired by Universal, Kerrigan showed no loyalty for the gesture the Flying A made to keep him happy and was lured to Universal with a substantial pay raise.

At right, J. Warren Kerrigan stars in *Samson* (Victor-Universal, released April 30, 1914). Although Universal was a single unified company, it continued to use the brand names of its founding members and to create new brands as well. The Victor brand was created for actress Florence Lawrence in 1912, and the Kerrigan films were added to the brand line when he signed with Universal. Below, Kerrigan (1879–1947) and director Otis Turner (1862–1918) are seen on the set of a 1915 Universal film. Turner, who was known as "the dean of moving picture directors," began his filmmaking career at the Selig Polyscope Company in Chicago in 1906. Kerrigan also started in Chicago, at the Essanay Film Manufacturing Company in 1910. Although he played manly roles, columnists warned fans that Kerrigan's "best girl" was his mother.

The MOVING PICTURE WEEKLY

FLORENCE LAWRENCE
FIRST AND MOST RECENT STAR OF THE UNIVERSAL
JANUARY 8, 1916
VOL. II   PRICE 5 CENTS   NO. 2

The January 6, 1916, issue of Universal's house organ celebrated the return of Florence Lawrence, "First and most recent star of the Universal." After becoming a household name with Carl Laemmle's IMP Company in 1909, Lawrence left to join the Lubin Manufacturing Company in Philadelphia. She stayed with Lubin for about a year and then came back to Laemmle and the newly organized Universal. According to Lawrence, her husband, actor-director Harry Solter (1874–1920), pushed her to be demanding and hold out for terms befitting her supposed status. She quit Universal, or was fired, in 1914 and later pleaded with Laemmle to let her return. Her 1916 comeback feature, *Elusive Isabel* (Bluebird-Universal, released May 15, 1916), was not a hit, and she drifted into bit parts and extra work. Lawrence committed suicide by ingesting ant paste in 1938.

Gender bending was the order of the day in *The Ring of Destiny* (Rex-Universal, released November 18, 1915), a two-reel comedy short featuring Edmund "Hoot" Gibson (right) and Cleo Madison (left), who also directed. Here Gibson offers Madison "the makings" for a hand-rolled cigarette, which he/she declines. Madison was one of several female directors at Universal in the 1910s. Others included Grace Cunard, Ida May Park, and Lois Weber.

New York Motion Picture Company ceded the 101 Bison logo when it withdrew from Universal but kept its popular Keystone comedy brand. To compete, Carl Laemmle created L-Ko (Lehrmann-Knockout) comedies. Here Laemmle (seated center) visits the set of *Cupid in a Hospital* (L-Ko/Universal, released January 6, 1915). Also seen are director Henry Lehrmann (with mustache and bow tie), character comic Hank Mann (at left, holding hat with his foot in a cast) and lead comic Billie Ritchie (center left, with bandage on his head).

Francis Ford (1882–1953), at left, was born Francis Feeney in Portland, Maine, and was the older brother of director John Ford. Around 1907, Ford landed a job at the Centaur Film Company in Bayonne, New Jersey, working with David Horsley and Al Christie. He later worked for Edison, Inc., and the American branch of Méliès Star Films. At Méliès, he became a director, specializing in Civil War dramas and Westerns. When Méliès abandoned American stories for South Seas dramas made on location, Ford moved to the New York Motion Picture Company in 1912. Always at odds with his supervisor, Thomas Ince, Ford opted to stick with Universal when Ince returned to NYMPC. Below, Ford and Grace Cunard prepare to shoot a scene along Cahuenga Boulevard in Hollywood in 1916.

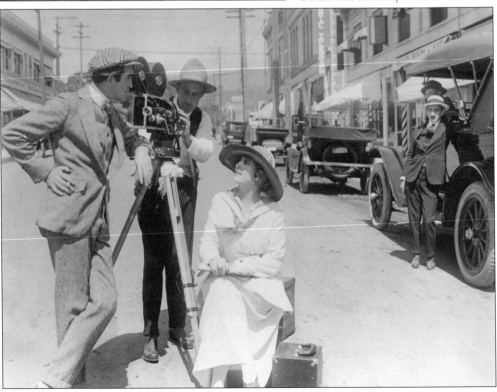

Press agents claimed Grace Cunard (1891–1967), at right, was a product of Paris, France, but she was born in Columbus, Ohio, as Harriet Mildred Jeffries and borrowed her stage name from the Grace and Cunard shipping lines. She became an actress with Francis Ford's unit at 101 Bison in 1912 after a career in stock and two years in pictures with Biograph, Kalem, Lubin, and finally the Yankee and Republic film companies. Grace Cunard became a valuable collaborator for Ford, writing scenarios and working as an associate director. Below, Ford and Cunard direct Eddie Polo in the 1915 serial *The Broken Coin* on location in Oxnard, California. Standing from left to right are cameraman Allen Siegler; Francis's brother, assistant director Jack Ford, later the Oscar-winning director John Ford; and assistant cameraman Ralph Merollo.

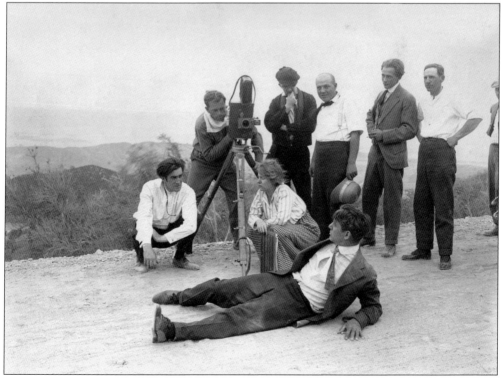

At left, Herbert Rawlinson (1885–1953) strikes an expansive pose atop his dressing room on the back side of the big outdoor stage at Universal City. Most actors love the spotlight, but their day in the sun is often short-lived. Rawlinson's career took an arc familiar to many silent film players: juvenile to leading man to star to character actor and finally to bit parts. Below, Universal encouraged visitors on the lot, realizing that publicity could be achieved and actors' appetites for attention satisfied. Here are three studio guests around 1916. The striped tent roof to the back left sits above a grandstand where crowds watched movies being made. Admission to Universal City cost 25¢, and the studio provided a free lunch.

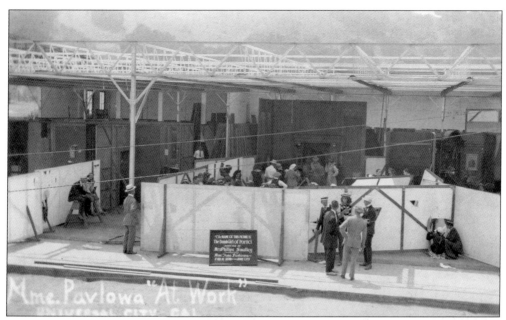

Mme. Pavlowa "At Work"

Not all actors were comfortable working under the watchful eye of strange fans. When Russian ballerina Anna Pavlova (1881–1931) made her first and only film, *The Dumb Girl of Portici* (released April 3, 1916), she insisted on a "closed set." The studio obliged by setting up muslin-covered flats around the unit's portion of the outdoor stage. The men seen at the stage entrance above appear to get the brush from an actor and a crewman, but a couple of enterprising women sneak a peak through a hole in the flats. The sign reads, "The Name of this picture is *The Dumb Girl of Portici* directed by Mrs. Phillips Smalley featuring Mme. Anna Pavlowa—It will be shown in your home city." At right, Mrs. Phillips Smalley, better known as Lois Weber (1881–1939), was generally regarded as the best female filmmaker of the silent era.

Universal added star power by raiding other companies for established players. Among those grabbed off was Ford Sterling (1883–1939), at left, who was noted for his "Dutch" comic portrayals and for playing the leader of the Keystone Kops. The Sterling Motion Picture Corporation was created, and Sterling was promised a cut of the profits. However, his tenure at Universal lasted only a few months. Hobart Bosworth was enticed from his own company, Bosworth, Inc. He had been making $125 a week with a promised 25-percent share of profits—but there were no profits. Laemmle offered Bosworth $350 a week to star and direct. Bosworth was relieved of his duties as director after his first Universal film, and his contract as an actor was not renewed when it expired. Below is a scene from *The Yacqi* (Bluebird-Universal, released March 19, 1916). Bosworth plays the title role. Goldie Colwell is the victim.

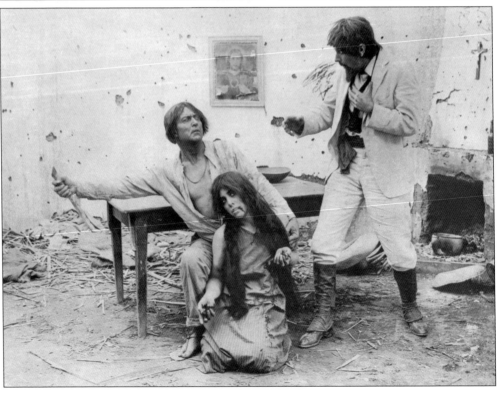

Universal provided a training ground for some of Hollywood's greatest directors—though they rarely stayed after becoming established. At right, Frank Lloyd and Helen Leslie are seen in *An Arrangement With Fate* (Laemmle-Universal, released March 21, 1915), which Lloyd also directed. He would go on to win Best Director Academy Awards for *The Divine Lady* (First National, 1929) and *Cavalcade* (Fox, 1933). Below, actor Robert Z. Leonard also moved behind the camera at Universal and went on to direct *Naughty Marietta* (M-G-M, 1935) with Jeanette MacDonald and Nelson Eddy, *A Tale of Two Cities* (M-G-M, 1935) starring Ronald Colman, and the Best Picture Oscar winner *The Great Ziegfeld* (M-G-M, 1936). Leonard is seen here on the Universal back lot directing Helen Ware in *Secret Love* (Bluebird-Universal, released January 31, 1916).

Mae Murray (1889–1965) languidly eyes a perched cockatoo as she pauses in writing a note with a feather quill pen in this oddly and unexpectedly sexual moment from *Princess Virtue* (Bluebird-Universal, released October 28, 1917). Murray began her career on stage as a dancer with Vernon Castle, joined the Ziegfeld Follies in 1908, and headlined the Follies in 1915. Although never a great actress, she was a great screen personality and is best remembered for her title role in director Erich von Stroheim's production of *The Merry Widow* (M-G-M, 1925). She married director Robert Z. Leonard, her third husband, the year after they made *Princess Virtue*, and they often worked together until their 1925 divorce.

Above, the movies' "Man of a Thousand Faces," Lon Chaney, served a lengthy apprenticeship at Universal, playing an assortment of supporting roles and villains. He quit the studio when the company refused him a $10 raise. Here Chaney is seen with mustache, wig, and plaid shirt in one of his villainous guises in *Quits* (Rex-Universal, released August 17, 1915). Arthur Shirley (left) plays the sheriff, and Roy McCray is wearing the long wig, second from right. Below, by the early 1920s, Lon Chaney was an established star when Universal wanted him for the title role in *The Hunchback of Notre Dame* (released September 6, 1923), but the grudge-holding actor held out for an additional $10 a week after he and Universal had agreed to terms. Nigel de Brulier played the Notre Dame priest.

Among the leading ladies developed by Universal was Patsy Ruth Miller (1904–1995), seen above as a female Tarzan in *Lorraine of the Lions* (released October 11, 1925). Educated in St. Louis, she came to Los Angeles on summer vacation with her parents in 1920 and was discovered by actress Alla Nazimova. She came to Universal in 1922. Below, although Mary Philbin (1902–1993) had the desire to become an actress, she got her chance in pictures because she was a neighbor and friend of Carl Laemmle's niece in Chicago. Best remembered for her over-the-top portrayal in 1925's *The Phantom of the Opera*, Philbin was capable of far more subtlety, as this scene from *Fool's Highway* (released March 1924) suggests. She worked with such leading directors as Erich von Stroheim and D. W. Griffith. Sound brought an end to her career.

Boxing great Jack Dempsey, seen above, made a series of two-reel comedy shorts for Universal in 1924. Dempsey poses with his director and the key technical people in his production unit. From left to right are cinematographer Clyde De Vinna, director Erle C. Kenton, Dempsey, and chief electrician, or "gaffer," Carl Gotham. Below, Reginald Denny gained attention in *The Leather Pushers*, a series of two-reel dramas about a pair of boxers, and that led to a feature with a fighting theme, *The Abysmal Brute* (released April 15, 1923), based on a novel by Jack London. Mabel Julienne Scott was the leading lady. Denny became Universal's leading light comedian in films like *Oh, Doctor!* (1925), *Skinner's Dress Suit* (1925), and *California Straight Ahead* (1926). He owned a well-known hobby shop in Hollywood for many years.

Erich von Stroheim earned his screen reputation as "The Man You Love to Hate" by playing variations of the "Hated Hun" in war movies churned out during World War I. At left is a gag shot of four-year-old child actor "Little Breezy" Eason, holding a pistol on Stroheim. The studio caption reads, "It takes a Marine to scare the Hun." Below, with "Hun" roles drying up, Stroheim persuaded Carl Laemmle to let him write, direct, and star in a film. The result was *Blind Husbands* (1919), a box-office hit, followed by another, *The Devil's Passkey* (1920). Stroheim's next picture, *Foolish Wives*, went severely over schedule and budget. Stroheim is seen in costume, directing *Foolish Wives* on the Universal lot with his wife, Valerie Germonprez, by his side.

Five

JEWELS AND SUPER JEWELS

In the nickelodeon era of the early 1910s, Universal was geared toward providing a complete film service to theater owners, who would often run three or four short films and change bills daily. At its production peak, Universal City was cranking out 36 reels (roughly nine hours) of completed film each week, mostly in the form of one- and two-reel shorts. To compete with distributors like the General Film Company (which released films of the Vitagraph, Edison, Biograph, Selig, Lubin, Essanay, and Kalem companies) and the Mutual Film Corporation (which distributed productions by Thanhouser, American, Keystone, Broncho, KayBee, and Gaumont), Universal maintained the brand names of its founding members and established new brand names as well to make exhibitors feel they were renting films from a number of different producers. Universal kept brand names like Rex, IMP, Powers, Nestor, and Bison alive and also created new "brands" like Sterling, Joker, Gold Seal, Victor, L-Ko, and Laemmle.

Even as feature films became the norm in the mid-1910s, Universal continued to brand its product. Standard features were released under the Broadway Features and later the Red Feather brand names, and the studio's more prestigious features were released by the Universal subsidiary Bluebird Photoplays, Inc.

By 1920, after Carl Laemmle bought the remaining interest of P. A. Powers, the studio sought to establish Universal Pictures as a single entity in the public's mind, although remnants of the branding policy continued into the 1920s with Mustang and Blue Streak Westerns.

Once he was in full control, Laemmle would head main-title cards with the words "Carl Laemmle presents," and the end-titles were often adorned with "Finis," French for "the end," and the words "It's a Universal!" and "Write me your opinion, Carl Laemmle, Universal City, Hollywood."

Still, Laemmle could not resist the temptation to differentiate the relative value of the Universal product to exhibitors. While a standard five- or six-reel feature may have gotten by with the simple declaration "It's a Universal!," the studio's better features, seven and eight reels in length, became known as Universal Jewels. When the company began turning out longer, bigger-budget specials, the designation "Jewel" did not seem to convey how truly extraordinary these big films were, so they were called "Super Jewels."

The above 1923 aerial view of Universal City, looking east, offers a sense of the studio layout. Visible on the back lot are the arches of the Notre Dame cathedral set. This was the only part actually built to scale. The top of the church was completed with a hanging miniature—a scale model placed near the camera in perspective with the set—that created a perfect illusion of the full structure. The site of the original Universal City is visible between the two hills at the upper left. Below, although Carl Laemmle packed the Universal payroll with his relatives, not all of them worked in the picture business. This photograph shows *The Hunchback of Notre Dame* sets and offers a good look at the egg ranch, which Carl Laemmle established for those in his family who were not suited for work in the movies.

Mythical city streets in the movies may have been paved with gold, but the streets of Universal City were still dirt roads in 1922, when the above view of the front lot, looking north, was taken. The detail below shows snow on the mountains and a 24-sheet poster for *Foolish Wives*, which was opening February 15, 1922, at the Mission Theater in Los Angeles. In another example of movie trickery, an art director has cleverly transformed one of the studio's practical buildings into the dockside offices of the South American Navigation Company by the application of some paint. The suggestion of a ship docked behind the building is created by the addition of a smokestack. The Technical Building in the front right had a nicely manicured lawn but needed painting seven years after it was completed.

Erich von Stroheim's *Foolish Wives* was an extravagant melodrama about a fake European count who finances his lavish lifestyle by seducing and then blackmailing gullible women. The action is set in Monte Carlo, and the studio spared no expense in re-creating the Monte Carlo Casino on the studio back lot. Here are two views, from roughly the same angle, of the set in daylight and at night. For the film, Stroheim and his movie cameramen avoided showing the brush-covered hill in the background. As *Foolish Wives* fell behind schedule and went over budget, Carl Laemmle turned lemons into lemonade by erecting a billboard in New York City touting the film as the first "million dollar picture."

At right, Irving Thalberg (1899–1936) poses with Carl Laemmle at the front door of the Universal City administration building about 1920. The twenty-one-year-old Thalberg was selected to supervise production at Universal. The opportunity may have arisen because Thalberg was considered marriageable material for Laemmle's daughter, Rosabelle. When Erich von Stroheim turned in a 24-reel cut of *Foolish Wives*, with a running time of nearly five hours, insisting it be screened in two parts over two evenings, Thalberg took the film away from the director and had it cut to 10 reels. Below, Stroheim and Miss DuPont play a scene on the Casino terrace. Shooting with two cameras side-by-side was common practice to create a second negative for foreign release, but Stroheim used the cameras to obtain different angles—a close-up for himself and another for Miss DuPont.

Above, Miss DuPont (1894–1973), née Patricia Hannon, played the spouse of an American ambassador in *Foolish Wives*. As in his previous films, Erich von Stroheim played the leading character, Count Wladislaw Sergius Karamzin, which presented a problem for the studio. Although Stroheim's films were profitable, his tendency to go over budget and unwillingness to deliver a film at a reasonable length made it impossible to fire him if he was appearing in the film as well as writing and directing. For his next production, *Merry-Go-Round* (released September 3, 1923), Irving Thalberg insisted that Stroheim not play a role. At left, Norman Kerry (1894–1956) was selected to play the "Stroheim role" in *Merry-Go-Round*. As Thalberg feared, Stroheim remained profligate and unrepentant. He was removed from *Merry-Go-Round* and replaced by director Rupert Juilan.

The newly completed Technical Building at Universal City (above), which contained the editorial department, is seen when the studio opened in March 1915. This is one of several souvenir picture postcards released in the 1910s depicting various scenes at the studio. Below, the editorial department at Universal City is seen in September 1916. According to a handwritten note on the back of the original photograph, the editorial staff included W. Gittens, chief; R. Brown, secretary; editors Earl Turner, Gilmore Walker, W. Blaine Pearson, Ralph Dixon, Dell Andrews, Grant Whytock, Lou Ostrow, ? Wallace, ? Younger, and ? Mohr; assistant editors Charles DeLong, Logan Pearson, Leo Bachman, Hank Knollmiller, Fred White, ? Grey, ? Anderson, and Fred ?; operators Carl Heindl, Abe Cohen, Slim Hough, ? Bennett, and "whatsisname"; and continuity clerks ? Johnson, ? Rothwell, and Sadie ?.

THE STORY OF THE
GREATEST FRIENDSHIP
IN THE HISTORY OF MAN

UNIVERSAL

PRESENTS

DAMON AND
PYTHIAS

THE WORLD'S PREMIER
DRAMATIC SPECTACLE

OFFERED IN SIX PARTS

ALHAMBRA

Majestic Theatre

LOS ANGELES

One Week com. Sun. MAR. 21

15c and 25c

Throughout its early history, Universal was primarily known as a producer of "bread and butter" pictures, making films intended for independent and small-town exhibitors. But the studio also produced a handful of special productions each year. These pictures were designed to play in more prestigious theaters and bring critical attention to the company. The first feature-length film completed at Universal City was *Damon and Pythias* (released November 23, 1914), based on a story by E. Bulwer Lytton and directed by Otis Turner.

The scene above from *Damon and Pythias* features Damon, played by William Worthington (standing left), greeting lovers Pythias and Calanthe, played by Herbert Rawlinson and Ann Little. The *Damon and Pythias* scenario was written by Ruth Ann Baldwin, who directed a dozen films for Universal in 1917. Although this Roman bathhouse setting is fairly detailed and elaborate, some of the "Roman" exteriors for the film looked like redressed buildings on the Universal City Western street. Below, the character Hermion, played by Cleo Madison, attempts to keep Damon from returning to Rome and certain arrest. Cleo Madison (1883–1964) was one of several women given the opportunity to become directors at Universal in the 1910s.

Above, Francis Ford (kneeling with back to camera) directs a scene with Grace Cunard from an unidentified 1915 Universal film. Stephen S. Norton (1877–1951) is cranking the camera. In its rush to turn out "product," Universal relied on reusable flats that could be erected and taken down quickly and provide serviceable, if not terribly convincing, interior settings. Below, between making shorts and serials, the team of Francis Ford and Grace Cunard also made some ambitious feature films like *The Campbells are Coming* (produced in December 1914 and January 1915 but not released until October 18, 1915). This rare snapshot shows Scottish troops storming an east Indian fort. The fender and front tire of a car are just visible at left, and the back of a female visitor to the back lot location can be seen on the right.

Although Universal experimented with electrical lights for illumination as early as 1913, the bulk of its work in the 1910s was shot outdoors in the abundant Southern California sunlight. The above photograph of a ballroom set from an unidentified film gives a good sense of the clean and evenly distributed light achievable on an outdoor stage with overhead muslin diffusers. Below, another large interior erected outdoors was the Gold Belt saloon and dance hall, built for *The Greater Law* (Bluebird-Universal, released July 16, 1917). Lynn F. Reynolds (seated right) was the director, and Clyde Cook was the cameraman. On the bench at left are leading lady Myrtle Gonzalez (1891–1918), Lawrence Payton, Jack Curtis (fourth from left), and George Hernandez. Gonzalez was a victim of the 1918 Spanish influenza epidemic.

Above, a truck unloads the undoubtedly hyperbolic "largest single delivery of lumber in the history of L. A." during construction of Stage 28 at Universal City in 1924. By the 1920s, with better film stocks and improvements in artificial lighting, it became practical to build "dark" stages in which filmmakers could effect more dramatic and subtle illumination of scenes. The interior of the Paris opera house, seen below, was built on Stage 28 for use in *The Phantom of the Opera*. The ornate opera house walls, partially visible at right, have remained standing on Universal City's Stage 28 since 1925 and are still in use today when a script calls for a lush theater setting.

Above, sophisticated lighting is seen in this moment from *Smouldering Fires* (released January 18, 1925), directed by Clarence Brown and photographed by Jackson Rose, ASC (American Society of Cinematographers). *Smouldering Fires* starred Malcolm McGregor (1892–1945) as a man in love with an older woman who is also his boss, played by Pauline Frederick (1883–1938). Below, this stunning art nouveau couturier shop scene is from Universal's *Fifth Avenue Models* (released April 26, 1925), directed by Svend Gade and photographed by Charles Stumar, ASC. It is another example of the blossoming artistic aspirations of Hollywood filmmakers in the 1920s. *Fifth Avenue Models* was Danish filmmaker Gade's first American film. He first gained international attention with his 1920 production of *Hamlet*, in which Asta Nielsen played the Prince of Denmark as a princess in drag.

Paul Fejos (1897–1963), at left, had a strange career path, working first in opera and avant-garde cinema in Europe before coming to America to work as a chemist with the Rockefeller Institute for Chemistry. He made another experimental film that caught the attention of Universal and then a handful of extraordinary films in the late 1920s, including *The Last Moment* (1927), *Lonesome* (1928), and the all-talkie *Broadway* (1929). He directed foreign-language versions of American films at M-G-M, then returned to Europe, where he made documentaries through the 1930s, before turning his attention to archaeology. Below, Fejos directs his first American film and actor Conrad Veidt as cinematographer Hall Mohr, ASC, lines up his camera on a focus chart during the production of *The Last Performance* (released November 2, 1927).

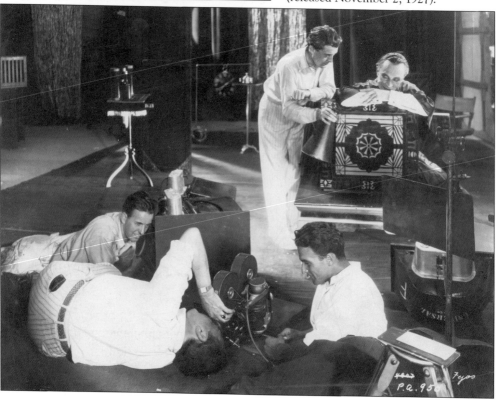

At right, German filmmaker Paul Leni (1885–1929) was noted for his expressionist films *Hintertreppe* (also known as *Backstairs*, 1921) and *Das Wachsfigurenkabinett* (also known as *Waxworks*, 1924) before he came to Hollywood in the late 1920s. He directed four visually striking films at Universal City—*The Cat and the Canary* (1927), *The Chinese Parrot* (1927, based on a Charlie Chan novel by Earl Derr Biggers), *The Man Who Laughs* (1928), and *The Last Warning* (1929)—before his death from blood poisoning. Below, Laura La Plante is menaced by a creeping hand in *The Cat and the Canary* (released September 9, 1927). Paul Leni's expressionist and atmospheric visual treatment of this 1922 play by John Willard helped set the visual style of the Universal horror cycle in the 1930s.

Above, the cast and crew of *The Cat and the Canary* pose for a photograph. Seated in front in chairs from left to right are Creighton Hale, Laura La Plante, Forrest Stanley, and Gertrude Astor. Paul Leni stands toward the left with his hand on Creighton Hale's chair; Tully Marshall is to the right of Leni; Martha Mattox is in the maid's uniform; character comedienne Flora Finch is seated to the right of Mattox; and cinematographer Gilbert Warrenton, ASC, stands at the top with an arm draped over the camera magazine. Below, on the set of *The Man Who Laughs* (released November 4, 1928), are Paul Leni at left with the raised megaphone; behind Leni is producer Paul Kohner; and behind Kohner is cinematographer Gilbert Warrenton, ASC. Second to the left in front is Conrad Veidt, standing with his hand over his mouth; and to the right of Veidt are Mary Philbin, Stuart Holmes, and Brandon Hurst.

Sound hit Hollywood hard. Warner Bros.' *The Jazz Singer* opened in October 1927, and barely a year later it was rare to see a silent film in a first-run theater. After the fluid visuals of the silent era, early talkies seemed rather like photographed plays. The dramatic scenes in *Broadway* (released May 27, 1929) were no exception, but director Paul Fejos compensated for the stagnant dialogue scenes with swooping visuals of the art moderne nightclub set where much of the action takes place. Universal built what came to be called "the *Broadway* crane" to make these shots possible. Above, the crew readies the crane on the partially lit set in preparation for a take. Below, the *Broadway* nightclub set is fully lit, with star Glenn Tryon and a bevy of chorus girls performing on the dance floor.

Above, beginning in 1926, Universal's *The Collegians* was a four-year, 32 installment—a series of two-reel shorts that followed a group of students through their freshman, sophomore, junior, and senior years at the imaginary Calford College. Here the cast of *The Collegians* presents Carl Laemmle Jr. with birthday congratulations in 1927. Junior is flanked by series stars Dorothy Gulliver and George Lewis. Arthur Lake is seated on the ground at left wearing a cap. Andy Devine wears the baseball uniform. Hoping that Carl Laemmle Jr. would prove as effective a producer as "boy genius" Irving Thalberg, Carl Laemmle elevated his son to head of production in 1929. Below, Carl Laemmle Jr., Carl Laemmle, and bandleader Paul Whiteman join in announcing Universal's "All Talking—All Singing—All Technicolor" production, *The King Of Jazz* (released April 20, 1930).

Carl Laemmle Jr. was not the only relative of "Uncle Carl" to be given a leg up in the picture business. At right, Julius Bernheim (1895–1970) came to the United States from Germany about 1910 and worked in the dark room at the IMP studios in New York. He became a production supervisor, what is today called a line producer. As with many of Carl Laemmle's relatives, Bernheim's movie career essentially ended when Laemmle sold the studio in 1936. Below, Reginald Denny (wearing cap with back to camera) shakes hands with Julius Bernheim in front of Stage 1 at Universal City as he embarks on a location road trip for *California Straight Ahead*, "A Tale of Highways and Byways" (released September 13, 1925). Director Harry Pollard is in the gray suit wearing glasses at right.

Above, Carl Laemmle's nephew Edward Laemmle (1887–1937) was a director of efficient low-budget pictures at Universal City. He is seen sitting at left in 1921 with leading lady Joey McCreery, cowboy star Art Acord, and supervisor of serials and short-reel features William Lord Wright. McCreery is best known as Marion Mack, the name she used as leading lady in Buster Keaton's 1927 feature *The General*. Below, the Laemmle relative with the most sustained success in Hollywood was William Wyler (1902–1981), seen here with Laura La Plante. He started as an assistant at Universal City in the early 1920s and went on to direct such classics as *Dodsworth* (1936), *Wuthering Heights* (1939), *The Best Years of Our Lives* (1946), and *Ben-Hur* (1959). Wyler won the Best Director Oscar three times.

Six

SIX-SHOOTIN' ROMANCE

When the Universal Film Manufacturing Company was formed in 1912, the most popular film genre with audiences here and abroad was the Western, and the popularity of "cowboy pictures" remained high with moviegoers until the 1950s.

There were advantages to making Westerns—they could be shot cheaply, mostly outdoors without need for lighting equipment, and the scenery that God created was the same whether the picture was developed by a "one-lung" producer on "poverty row" or a major studio like M-G-M, Fox, or Paramount.

Without a theater chain of its own, Universal catered to smaller independent theater owners, often located outside the big cities—and these exhibitors loved Westerns, not only because they were popular with young and old but because they could be rented cheaply. Often five-reel Westerns could be booked for as little as $10 a day, leaving the theater owner with a wider profit margin than he would have showing films with big-name box-office stars and higher rental fees.

While Carlo Gozzi and his later disciple Gorges Polti averred that there are 36 basic dramatic situations, those less attuned to the fine points of Westerns might argue that there are only two or three basic Western plots: the Indians attack, the cavalry arrives in the nick of time; the cattle rancher's land is about to be lost to an unscrupulous villain because of debt, disputed water rights, or boundaries; or the sudden arrival of sheepherders and their flocks. But through it all, justice—in the guise of a lone cowboy who rides into the middle of the plot—will prevail. The one real requirement is that there's got to be a girl. No matter that she is the only eligible bachelorette in the territory with her choice of any man in town; she will end up in the arms of the cowboy hero for one brief clinch before the final fade out. For the Western aficionado, however, the plot is secondary to the broad vistas of the desert landscapes and the sun hitting the trails of dust as galloping horsemen thunder down the trail.

From J. Warren Kerrigan in 1913 to Audie Murphy in 1963, Universal relied heavily on its cowboy stars to bring in a steady stream of income and offset the losses sometimes generated by its "prestige" pictures.

Above, Harry Carey was Universal's most popular Western star in the 1910s and early 1920s. He played a rather somber character, very much in the mode of screen cowboy William S. Hart. In the Carey unit at Universal City in 1916 are, from left to right, (first row) Joe Rickson, Neal Hart, Harry Carey, Olive Fuller Golden (later Carey's wife), director George Marshall, and an unidentified cowboy; (second row) unidentified, Pedro Leone, and Bud Osborne; (third row) two unidentified, assistant director Teddy Brooks, Bill Gillis, and Jim Corey. Below, Harry Carey is seen in *The Freeze-Out* (released April 9, 1921), one of the last pictures directed by John Ford at Universal before he signed with the Fox Film Corporation.

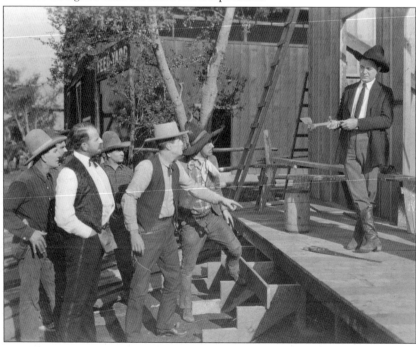

Above, Joe Rickson (1880–1958) was one of the real-life cowboys who made his way to Universal City in the movies' early days. He is seen here in *An Indian Eclipse* (Nestor-Universal, released July 29, 1914). Rickson "won" his wife in a roping contest with a rival cowboy—an event that was fictionalized by Western star Tom Mix in *Roping a Bride* (Selig Polyscope, 1915) and its remake, *Roping a Sweetheart* (Selig Polyscope, 1916). Rickson starred in a few films before settling into supporting roles. Below, Joe Rickson took this tumble in *The Committee on Credentials* (released July 8, 1916), directed by George Marshall, who went on to helm such classics as *Destry Rides Again* (Universal, 1939), *The Ghost Breakers* (Paramount, 1940), and *Murder He Says* (Paramount, 1945).

Above, Universal's most popular Western star was Edmund "Hoot" Gibson (1892–1962), shown at right in a scene from *"In Wrong" Wright* (released October 30, 1920). Gibson was wintering with the Dick Stanley Wild West Show in Los Angeles when he began his movie career with the Selig Polyscope Company in 1909. He got the nickname "Hoot" when he was a delivery boy for the Owl Drug Company. Below, Gibson listens in on a take through Universal's newfangled sound equipment. In 1930, Gibson signed a deal to produce his own pictures for Universal but was let go in 1931 during the industry-wide presumption that Westerns were dead. Small-town theaters weren't yet wired for sound, and first-run houses didn't play cowboy pictures.

Jack Hoxie (1885–1965), at right, was another popular Universal Western star from 1923 through 1927. He made more money in personal appearances and gave up the screen in 1933 to become a circus and rodeo performer. Like most of the early screen cowboys, Hoxie had ranch experience. Below, Hoxie gets ready to do some Roman riding for his film *Two-Fisted Jones* (released December 6, 1925). The hard-as-nails cowboys made ideal stuntmen in early Hollywood. They had an informal organization they called "The 400," which monitored the skills of would-be stunt performers in order to avoid getting themselves killed working with amateurs. Jack Hoxie's brother Al Hoxie attempted to cash in on Jack's popularity by starring in a handful of cheap, independently produced oaters in the late 1920s.

Carl Laemmle and Ted Wells greet Vonceil Viking at Universal City after her 120-day horseback ride from New York to California. Laemmle promised her a role in a Western with Wells (1899–1948). Instead, Laemmle made good on his promise by putting Viking in a 1928 two-reeler with Edmund Cobb called *The Fighting Forester*. It was her only film. She was killed in an automobile accident on December 2, 1929, at age 27. Below is a scene from *The Crimson Canyon* (released on October 14, 1928) starring Ted Wells and Lotus Thompson (1906–1963). Wells signed with Universal in 1927. He had a short-lived starring career and played mostly bit parts in the sound era. Under his real name, John Wells, he first worked in films in an abortive 1925 project for the short-lived Thomas C. Regan Studio.

When the market for Westerns revived, Universal courted the king of Hollywood cowboys, Tom Mix (1880–1940). In the late 1920s at Fox, Mix was making pictures with budgets of $175,000 and 30-day shooting schedules. At Universal, the Mix budgets were trimmed to $90,000 and the shooting schedules cut to 10 days. Still, the Universal Mix pictures were leagues ahead of the average independent Westerns that were cranked out for $7,000 to $10,000 on six-day schedules. At right, director Albert S. Rogell visits Tom Mix on the set of *The Texas Bad Man* in 1932. Rogell directed Mix's second Universal talkie, *The Rider of Death Valley* (released April 24, 1932). Below, Tom brings in some stagecoach robbers on the Universal City Western street in his first talkie, *Destry Rides Again* (released April 17, 1932).

Ken Maynard (1895–1973), at left, was established as a first-rank cowboy star with a series of slick Westerns for First National Pictures between 1926 and 1928. A former circus cowboy noted for stunt riding, Maynard did two stints at Universal, during the 1929–1930 season and 1933–1934. As with Hoot Gibson's later films for the studio, Maynard was given his own company and money was advanced for each picture, with Maynard being responsible for delivering on budget. Below, Tom Mix's closest rival in the silent era was Buck Jones, who was signed by Universal when Mix left in 1933. Here Buck reviews the home chapter of the Buck Jones Rangers from Belvedere Gardens, Los Angeles, with Carl Laemmle in 1934. The poster on the billboard touts Universal's latest film, *Embarrassing Moments* (released September 1, 1934).

Seven

OH, THE HORROR!

Universal's most enduring cinematic legacy is its highly regarded "horror cycle" of the early 1930s. The films have been reissued theatrically numerous times; packaged for early television as *Shock Theater*; remade; spun off; marketed to home video on VHS tape, laser disc, and DVD; and it is absolutely certain that as new technologies emerge, Universal will repurpose their Frankenstein, Dracula, Mummy, Invisible Man, and Werewolf pictures for new audiences well into the future.

The studio's monster movies captured the imagination of Depression-era audiences when they first hit the screen. The evil characters bent on the destruction of mankind were seen as a metaphor for the very real and terrifying economic forces that gripped the population.

But Universal's monsters also had their sympathetic side—Frankenstein's monster yearning for a mate, Larry Talbot's tortured efforts to keep from killing his beloved when he transforms into the Wolfman—which made the audience root for these characters even as they were repelled by their disfigured looks and evil ways.

Films like *Bride of Frankenstein* and *The Old Dark House*, black comedies really rather than out-and-out thrillers, brought humor to the horror and made these films highly enjoyable as well as creepy.

Horror films helped offset the losses on some of Universal's big-budget flops, but with their expressionist art direction and long hours required for makeup, visual, and special effects, these films, popular as they were, required a broad market to be successful.

When Great Britain placed a ban on the importation and screening of horror films in the mid-1930s, the future of the genre was in doubt as a sizable portion of the market was cut off. The ban was ultimately relaxed, but fearful producers were reluctant to spend big money on horror pictures for fear that another ban would limit their profit-making potential. World War II also limited foreign sales, and though Universal continued to make horror films based on their classic characters through the 1940s, they were shot on B-picture budgets and intended largely for children.

Known for its horror films in the 1930s, Universal actually had a tradition in the silent era with pictures like *The Hunchback of Notre Dame* (1923) and *The Phantom of the Opera* (1925). Above, Carl Laemmle and visitors, on the stairs to the left in the background, watch as director Rupert Julian gives instructions to his off-camera crew. Norman Kerry and Mary Philbin stand on the stairs. Below, Norman Kerry and Mary Philbin share an exchange of pleasantries with Carl Laemmle as Rupert Julian rehearses an army of extras for the masked ball sequence in *The Phantom of the Opera*. This sequence was photographed in the two-color Technicolor process.

Not wanting to diminish the shock value of Lon Chaney's makeup for his role as Erik, the Phantom, early publicity photographs, like the one above, were released with the Phantom's head out of frame or "whited out" to conceal his horrific visage. Below, Lon Chaney wore an idealized porcelain mask to conceal his appearance in the early scenes. When he kidnaps the opera singer, Christine Daae, and carries her to his hidden lodgings beneath the Paris opera, curiosity gets the better of her and she sneaks up behind and unmasks the Phantom in one of the screen's first truly terrifying moments. *The Phantom of the Opera* was a troubled production. An early preview did not go well, and revisions were ordered. Edward Sedgwick directed the new scenes. Later the picture was revised again with Lois Weber reworking the existing footage and titles.

Although horrific elements existed in Universal pictures like *The Cat and the Canary* (1927) and *The Man Who Laughs* (1928), Universal's horror cycle really got underway with *Dracula* (released February 14, 1931) starring Bela Lugosi (1882–1956), seen at left. The screen version was based on Hamilton Deane and John L. Balderston's 1927 stage adaptation of the 1897 Bram Stoker novel. Lugosi starred in the Broadway production; and Edward van Sloan, who played Von Helsing in the film, also reprised his stage role. Below, the United States was feeling the effects of the October 1929 Wall Street crash by 1931, and *Dracula* proved to be a real shot in the arm for the fortunes of Universal Pictures. The picture drew record crowds to the 5,920-seat Roxy Theater at 153 West Fiftieth Street, between Sixth and Seventh Avenues, New York City.

Record crowds at Roxy showing of "DRACULA". The lines four abreast waiting to get into the "next" performance. The Box-office told the story!

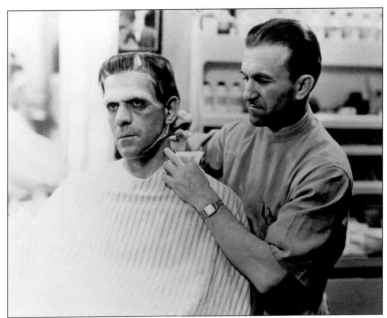

The second of Carl Laemmle Jr.'s horror films was an adaptation of Mary Shelley's 1818 novel, *Frankenstein* (released November 21, 1931). Above, the monster, played by Boris Karloff, née William Henry Pratt (1887–1969), became an iconic movie character, revived in sequels, cartoons, and even in television series like *The Munsters*. The makeup was created by Jack Pierce, née Janus Piccoulas (1889–1968), a former actor who became a makeup artist in the late 1920s. Here Pierce applies makeup to Karloff. The transformation required four hours. Below, other iconic elements in *Frankenstein* were the glowing and sputtering electrical devices that Dr. Henry Frankenstein used to bring his monster to life. The electrical props were created by Kenneth Strickfadden (1896–1984), and for years such devices were required equipment in Hollywood films whenever a mad scientist entered a laboratory.

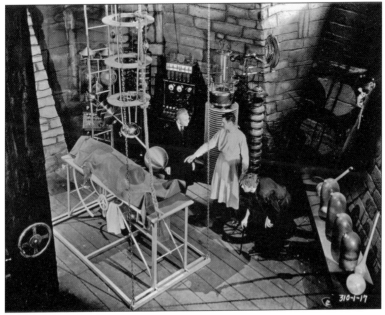

What made Universal horror films so popular is that they dealt with adult themes even as they thrilled with melodramatic absurdity. The best of them, *Frankenstein* (1931), *The Old Dark House* (1932), and *The Invisible Man* (1933), were directed by James Whale (1889–1957), who brought a tongue-in-cheek sense of humor to his monster movies. Above, always the proper Englishman, James Whale takes afternoon tea with fellow Britisher Ernest Thesiger, who played the fruity Dr. Pretorius in *Bride of Frankenstein* (released April 22, 1935), one Hollywood sequel that was actually superior to the original. By the mid-1930s, Boris Karloff (below) was so well known he was referred to by last name only, on posters for *The Invisible Ray* (released January 20, 1936), while Bela Lugosi was reduced to supporting status, with his name printed half the size of Karloff's.

Eight

SIGNING OFF

In 1929, when Carl Laemmle Jr. turned 21, his father gave him the studio as a birthday present—figuratively, anyway. Junior Laemmle was put in charge of production at Universal City. Hollywood wags couldn't resist smirking that "the son also rises," and Junior was often criticized for overspending on his pet projects as he paid little attention to the studio's slate of program pictures, which were often supervised by Carl Laemmle's son-in-law, Stanley Bergerman, or Universal old-timer Henry McRae.

For all the cracks and criticism, however, Carl Laemmle Jr. did produce some remarkable films in his seven years as head of production. *The King of Jazz, All Quiet on the Western Front, Dracula, Frankenstein, The Mummy, Counselor at Law, Remember Last Night?, The Invisible Man, Back Street, Waterloo Bridge, Little Man What Now?, The Good Fairy, Imitation of Life, Show Boat,* and other first-rate pictures silenced critics of the studio's past reliance on low-budget fare.

But a number of these pictures did not perform as well as hoped for, and there was pressure from the low-budget side as well as several independent producers gathered together to form Republic Pictures in 1935. The new company provided stiff competition for Universal with its traditional customer base.

Universal had always turned out one or two Super Jewels each year, and the market had been able to absorb these films. Harry Cohn over at Columbia successfully followed this same path—concentrating on program pictures, with a couple of special attractions to add to his studio's prestige. But Carl Laemmle Jr.'s ambitions outpaced the ability of Universal's core customers to absorb a steady stream of more expensive product.

In the late 1920s, Universal had nearly gone bust over two big pictures, *Uncle Tom's Cabin* and *Show Boat*. Not only were they over budget, but both were silent films made just as the public was going crazy for talkies. A recorded musical score and sound effects were added to *Uncle Tom's Cabin*, and half of *Show Boat* was reshot with "goat glanded" talking sequences, but these efforts only added to the costs without making the pictures more viable at the box office.

In 1935, Carl Laemmle Jr. decided to remake *Show Boat*. The picture would be his triumph and lead to his ruination.

Hollywood's moguls seemed obsessed with telling their stories in "puff-piece" books like *The House that Shadows Built* (1928) about Adolph Zukor and Paramount Pictures, *The Film Finds Its Tongue* (1929) about the Warner brothers, and *Upton Sinclair Presents William Fox* (1933). Carl Laemmle commissioned English playwright and poet John Drinkwater to write his story. The result was *The Life and Adventures of Carl Laemmle*, published in 1930 by G. P. Putnam's Sons in the United States and Heinemann in Great Britain. Drinkwater was known for biographical plays like *Abraham Lincoln* (1918), *Mary Stuart* (1921), and *Oliver Cromwell* (also 1921), but his biography of the head of Universal is a turgid bore padded with syrupy asides to the reader. This window display of the book at the Carnegie Hall Book Shop in New York City attracted little attention from the public.

In the movies, the audience only sees what the camera sees, and odd juxtapositions can occur on a studio lot. In the foreground is the bare skeleton of a tree in what is supposed to be "no man's land" in World War I, but in the background to the left, leafy palm trees sway. The *Broadway* crane was put into service again to help achieve vivid overhead angles and moving camera shots for Universal's production of *All Quiet on the Western Front* (released August 24, 1930). Based on the novel by Erich Maria Remarque, the film told the story of the Great War from the perspective of German soldiers in the trenches. Highly controversial (the book had been briefly banned in the United States), the film directed by Lewis Milestone earned Oscars for Best Director and Best Picture.

Erich von Stroheim believed that ZaSu Pitts (1894–1963) was one of the screen's great dramatic actresses, and her performances in Stroheim's *Greed* (1924) and *The Wedding March* (1928) supported his judgment. But Pitts also excelled in comic roles and was often cast as a nervous Nellie with bird-like gestures. Above, one of her last opportunities in a dramatic role came as the mother of Lew Ayres in *All Quiet on the Western Front*. Preview audiences laughed when she came on screen. This is a rare photograph of her work in the film. All of her scenes were reshot. Below, Beryl Mercer (1882–1939), seen with Lew Ayres and Marion Clayton, was noted for playing mother roles and replaced ZaSu Pitts in *All Quiet on the Western Front*. Today Mercer's whiny performance is one of the film's few weaknesses.

Above, in *All Quiet on the Western Front*, Louis Wolheim (1880–1931) played Sergeant Katczinsky, mentor to young Paul Baumer, played by Lew Ayres. A former math teacher and fluent in several languages, Wolheim was told by actor Lionel Barrymore, "With that face you could make a fortune in the theater." Wolheim kept busy in films from 1914 on and made his biggest splash in Eugene O'Neill's 1922 play *The Hairy Ape*. Below, a silent bit as a dying French soldier in *All Quiet on the Western Front* was the last screen role for Raymond Griffith (1895–1957). Respiratory diphtheria damaged Griffith's vocal chords, and he spoke in a hoarse whisper. A star in silent films, Griffith attempted to recapture his stardom in two talkie shorts but turned to producing when it was clear his voice wasn't suited for sound.

Above, despite earlier problems with director Erich von Stroheim, Carl Laemmle was persuaded by producer Paul Kohner to sign the filmmaker to direct a sound remake of *Foolish Wives*. The project was aborted, but Stroheim posed with Laemmle in a number of 1931–1932 publicity photographs. Here Laemmle and Stroheim greet Austrian Archduke Leopold (left) at Universal City. With his son in charge of production, much of Carl Laemmle's time was taken up with ceremonial affairs. The photograph below commemorates a 1935 visit to Universal City by Czech violinist and composer Jan Kubelík (1880–1940). From left to right are Roberto Fanti, Universal's representative in Rome, Italy; actor Francis Lederer (1899–2000), born František Lederer near Prague; Carl Laemmle; Kubelík's son, conductor and composer Rafael Jeroným Kubelík (1914–1996); and Jan Kubelík.

At right, another visitor to Universal City was famed University of Notre Dame football coach Knute Rockne (1888–1931). Carl Laemmle posed with Rockne, who was signed to make six football shorts in Universal's *All American Sports* series, produced by Christy Walsh. Undoubtedly Rockne was slated to appear in the six films, but only five were made and all were released months after Rockne's March 31, 1931, death in a plane crash. Exploiting the publicity value of the coach's name, Universal credited Rockne as the writer of the five shorts. Below, Universal also cashed in on Rockne's fame with the feature film *The Spirit of Notre Dame* (released October 13, 1931). J. Farrell MacDonald (bare chested), who bore a resemblance to Rockne, played the coach; and renowned athlete Jim Thorpe, fourth from right, was also in the film.

At left, Carl Laemmle Jr. (right) and Fox West Coast Theaters head Charles Skouras are seen before the premiere of Universal's *Back Street* (released December 30, 1932). Based on Fanny Hurst's novel, *Back Street* starred Irene Dunne as "the other woman" and John Boles as her married lover. The story was remade twice, in 1941 with Margaret Sullavan and Charles Boyer and again in 1961 with Susan Hayward and John Gavin. Below, a crowd waits to get into the Palace Theater on Randolph Street in Chicago to see *The Good Fairy* (released February 18, 1935). Based on a play by Ferenc Molnár and directed by William Wyler, *The Good Fairy* was a prestigious picture for Universal, but the word on the street was that Junior Laemmle spent too much on pictures that would never recoup their costs.

Above, studio workers and guests gather on a sound stage to celebrate the 20th anniversary of Universal City in 1935. The studio caption reads, "Carl Laemmle greets studio employees who have been with the firm 20 years or more. In the immediate foreground left to right are Edward Laemmle, director; Harry McPheeters, electrician; Martin Murphy, production manager; Ella O'Neil; Henry McRae; Maurice Pivar, editorial supervisor; Archie Hall, technical chief, and Scott R. Beal, director and former actor. More than 40 studio employees who attended the opening of Universal City, March 15, 1915, are still daily active at the big plant." Below, reunited at the Universal City 20th anniversary party are Grace Cunard and Francis Ford. Once writers, directors, and stars of their own films, both Cunard and Ford were doing bit parts and extra work in 1935.

By late 1935, Universal was in financial trouble, and Carl Laemmle borrowed $750,000 from Standard Capital, a financial group headed by J. Cheever Cowdin and Charles R. Rogers. As collateral, Laemmle gave Standard Capital a purchase option on his stock in Universal. As the schedule of Carl Laemmle Jr.'s production of *Show Boat* dragged on, Laemmle was forced to borrow an additional $300,000 in February 1936 to keep the studio going. Above, director James Whale (pointing) and cinematographer John J. Mescall, ASC, both to the right of the camera, prepare to shoot a scene for the 1936 version of *Show Boat*. Below is the wedding of Magnolia Hawks (played by Irene Dunne) and Gaylord Ravenal (Allan Jones) in *Show Boat* (released May 14, 1936). Looking on from left to right are Sammy White; Charles Winninger, who originated the role of Capt. Andy Hawks in the 1927 Broadway production; and Queenie Smith.

On March 14, 1936, Standard Capital unexpectedly paid $1.5 million to exercise its purchase option and delivered the $4-million balance on April 2, 1936, forcing Carl Laemmle out of Universal. Carl Laemmle Jr. resigned in late April after the first public screening of *Show Boat*. The New Universal signed teenage singing sensation Deanna Durbin to a contract on June 15, 1936. Above is a scene from *One Hundred Men and a Girl* (released September 5, 1937) with, from left to right, Adolphe Menjou, Deanna Durbin, and Mischa Auer, which was so successful that it is said to have saved the studio. At right is Durbin, who was born on December 4, 1921, in Winnipeg, Canada, as Edna Mae Durbin. In the 12 years she spent at the New Universal, she made 21 films that were considered "mortgage lifters" for the revitalized company.

Above, the studio caption reads, "Screen veterans and attractive newcomers mingled at the 30th anniversary of Carl Laemmle's entrance into motion pictures yesterday [February 24, 1936] at Universal studios. From left to right: Mike Marco, Jesse L. Lasky, Gloria Stuart, Noah Beery Jr., Irene Dunne, William Koenig, May Robson, Commodore J. Stuart Blackton, Diana Gibson, Fred Beetson, Carle Laemmle, Carl Laemmle Jr., Binnie Barnes, Rupert Hughes, Cesar Romero, Cecil B. DeMille, Mrs. Stanley Bergerman (Rosabelle Laemmle), Hobart Bosworth, Stanley Bergerman. In the rear Charlie Murray, John King and other film notables." Below, this picture of Carl Laemmle, his son Carl Laemmle Jr., his daughter Rosabelle Laemmle Bergerman, and her two children, Carol Bergerman and Stanley Bergerman Jr., was taken in September 1938 by a Santa Fe Railway photographer, almost exactly a year to the day before Carl Laemmle's death on September 24, 1939, at age 72.

UNIVERSAL STUDIOS UNIVERSAL CITY, CAL. 257

Although the facade of the Universal City studio administration building was enlarged and remodeled to make it seem a bit more up to date, the film laboratory and commissary buildings look much as they did on March 15, 1915, in this photograph taken in the 1940s. These buildings stood until the early 1960s, when they were torn down to make room for Universal City Plaza. Today all that survives of the original Universal City buildings is a stained-glass window bearing the Universal logo, which stood above the main entrance of the old administration building.

Discover Thousands of Local History Books Featuring Millions of Vintage Images

Arcadia Publishing, the leading local history publisher in the United States, is committed to making history accessible and meaningful through publishing books that celebrate and preserve the heritage of America's people and places.

Find more books like this at
www.arcadiapublishing.com

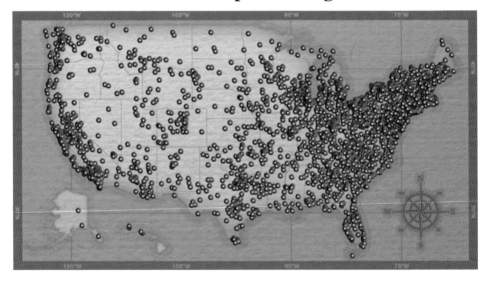

Search for your hometown history, your old stomping grounds, and even your favorite sports team.